You
Are the
Corporate
Executive

GREAT DECISIONS

YOU
ARE THE
CORPORATE
EXECUTIVE

Nathan Aaseng

The Oliver Press, Inc.
Minneapolis

$

The Oliver Press, Inc.
Charlotte Square
5707 West 36th Street
Minneapolis, MN 55416-2510

The publisher wishes to thank the Pavek Museum of Broadcasting,
St. Louis Park, Minnesota, for graciously allowing items in its
collection to be photographed for this book. These items appear
on pages 66, 68, 72, 75, and 77.

Library of Congress Cataloging-in-Publication Data

Aaseng, Nathan.
You are the corporate executive / Nathan Aaseng.
p.   cm.—(Great decisions)
Includes bibliographical references and index.
    Summary: Examines eight crucial business decisions of the
twentieth century.
ISBN 1-881508-35-8 (lib. bdg.)
1. Chief executive officers—Juvenile literature. 2. Decision-mak-
ing—Juvenile literature. 3. Executive ability—Juvenile literature.
[1. Chief executive officers. 2. Decision making. 3. Leadership.]
I. Title. II. Series.
HD38.2.A22   1996
658.4—dc20   96-4570
                                                  CIP
                                                  AC

ISBN: 1-881508-35-8
Great Decisions VII
Printed in the United States of America

03 02 01 00 99 98 97   8 7 6 5 4 3 2 1

CONTENTS

Richly decorated offices often reflect the prestige of top corporate executives.

INTRODUCTION

The position of corporate executive shines as a symbol of success in the business world. When you sit in an executive's chair at a major corporation, you have made it big. You command both wealth and power. You call the shots.

Although that role may sound attractive, there is another side to the story. Along with wealth and power comes enormous responsibility.

In this book, that burden of responsibility rests squarely on you. As one of the top officials of a large company, you must confront problems with millions, sometimes billions, of dollars at stake. The decisions you make could save or destroy a respected and established company. The livelihoods of hundreds, perhaps even thousands, of employees are in your hands.

The risks you face are many, and the consequences of your actions may be disastrous. In the 1950s, the Ford Motor Company lost an enormous amount of money because of an executive decision to produce the Edsel, a car that the American public was not willing to buy.

The infamous Edsel, a car that never gained customer interest, lives on as a reminder that even successful companies can sometimes fail in the marketplace.

Because the country had suffered economically following World War I, the head of Montgomery Ward believed the United States was headed for similar tough economic times after World War II. As a result, during the seven-year period from 1945 to 1952, Ward's built no new stores. Meanwhile, its main rival—Sears—took the opposite approach and built more than 100 new stores. Sears made the right decision. It grew into one of the world's largest corporations while Montgomery Ward fell from prominence.

By making wise business decisions, executives and
their companies can really pile up the cash!

In the 1970s, RCA executives approved a research and development project for a home videodisk player. After years of work and $150 million in development costs, their SelectaVision product came on the market in the early 1980s. The company had anticipated sales of 500,000 units in its first year. Instead, RCA struggled for three years before it reached that number. Customers rejected the product in favor of other types of home video systems that, unlike the SelectaVision, could record television programs. As a result of the negative consumer reaction to SelectaVision, RCA had to abandon the product and swallow the costs.

None of these mistakes was easy to anticipate, and there is no sure-fire formula for predicting which course of action a company should take. But someone has to make that decision and take responsibility for the consequences. In this book, that someone is you.

This book presents eight difficult situations that eight prominent corporations have faced. While the situations may be stressful, keep in mind Robert Heller's observation in *The Decision Makers* that "crises give heroes the opportunity for heroism." Weigh the options carefully before choosing your course of action and test your instincts as you try to steer your company away from disaster and into prosperity.

1

PARKER PENS
BALLPOINT BREAKTHROUGH
1945

For several decades, your company has been the sales leader among fountain-pen manufacturers. The traditional fountain pen contains a reservoir of ink that flows into a writing tip. But recently one of your competitors has introduced a new type of writing instrument that has dramatically changed the pen industry. Customers are flocking to buy this new "ballpoint." Virtually every other pen manufacturer is now scrambling to get its own ballpoint pens into the market.

At the moment, the Parker Pen Company does not offer a ballpoint pen. How will you respond to the challenge of this new technology?

George S. Parker, the founder of the Parker Pen Company, ran his business by the philosophy, "Make something better and people will buy it."

BACKGROUND

The Parker Pen Company came about as a result of one man's commitment to quality. In 1888, schoolteacher George Parker of Janesville, Wisconsin, decided to distribute pens as a way of earning some extra income. But because the pens that he sold leaked and broke frequently, Parker soon regretted his decision.

Although he did not manufacture the pens, honest George Parker felt responsible to his customers. He therefore agreed to repair any malfunctioning pen that he had sold. Before long, Parker was spending all of his spare time fixing pens.

From his many hours of repairing pens, Parker knew that he could easily design and build better pens than those that were currently on the market. So, in 1888, he left his teaching career and started the Parker Pen Company. Running his company with a bull-headed

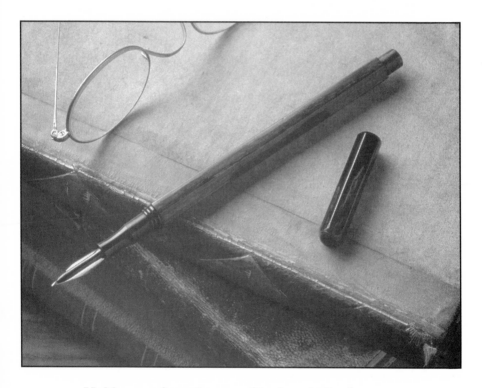

Unlike most fountain pens of its day, the Lucky Curve, Parker's first major success, did not leak ink on the fingers of the writer.

commitment to quality, Parker insisted that all of the company's advertising claims be completely honest. In order to operate a successful business under that rule, Parker realized that he had to build the best pens in the world.

Parker was both a perfectionist and a tinkerer. During his relentless search for a flawless pen design, he invented many new features. The U.S. government approved dozens of patents for his innovations, and his successors have continued that dedication to quality. By the early 1940s, the company held more than 150 patents.

Architects, designers, and artists have come to appreciate Parker's demanding standards of quality. They have voted the Parker 51, introduced four years ago in 1941, as one of the five best-designed products of all time. Commitment to quality has paid off in the international marketplace as well. Parker is currently the world's leading seller of pens.

But now, in 1945, Parker's dominant position has come under attack from the ballpoint pen. Ballpoints use a small, rotating steel ball bearing as the writing point. They are easier to use, require no cleaning or maintenance, and can be produced more cheaply than fountain pens. To highlight its versatility, one competitor advertises its ballpoint as "the pen that writes under water."

The ballpoint pen was actually invented in 1881, more than half a century ago. But their poor quality and manufacturing problems prevented them from challenging fountain pens until now. Your competitors say they have solved those difficulties, and the public has gone into a buying frenzy over the new ballpoint pen.

General Dwight D. Eisenhower, commander of the Allied forces, used two Parker 51 pens to sign the documents that ended World War II in Europe.

THE DECISION IS YOURS.

As a corporate executive of the Parker Pen Company, how will you respond to the new ballpoint technology?

Option 1 Meet the challenge by producing a ballpoint pen immediately.

Your competitors are making a fortune on their ballpoint pens. They are asking up to $15 each for these inexpensively made pens and are selling all they can manufacture. How long do you think you can stay in business if you sit on the sidelines while competitors rake in such huge profits on their sales?

The Parker Pen Company is now one of the few major pen manufacturers that has not jumped into the ballpoint-pen market. Is Parker going to be the only company so stodgy and stubborn that it refuses to recognize the ballpoint as the pen of the future?

Producing a ballpoint pen is not a complicated and difficult task. The technology is fairly simple. The only reason that ballpoint pens have not challenged fountain pens up until now is that there was a lack of suitable materials. But the engineers who produced equipment for the military during World War II made great improvements in the techniques for grinding ball bearings, and these new techniques make it possible to produce a far superior ballpoint pen. Recently developed inks that dry faster and thus smudge less have also improved the quality of ballpoint pens.

Parker can easily put together a ballpoint pen similar to those now on the market. It must do so immediately before its competitors dominate the vast new ballpoint-pen market.

Option 2 **Set a five-year target for producing ballpoint pens.**

Because ballpoint pens are obviously the wave of the future, the Parker Pen Company has no choice but to go along with the trend. But while these pens may be a hot-selling item, the current ballpoints are far from perfect. In fact, many of them simply do not work.

When the novelty of the new pens wears off, manufacturers will have to prove their claims that ballpoint pens are easier to use and more reliable than fountain pens. It will be difficult for those who have manufactured shoddy merchandise to keep old customers and attract others to their product.

Your company can afford to wait a few years before joining the ballpoint-pen race. That way, you will have the time to develop a reliable ballpoint pen that will be superior to those of your competitors. But you must set a five-year target now in order to convince your designers and engineers of the urgency of getting a ballpoint product into the market.

Option 3 **Stay out of the ballpoint-pen business for as long as is necessary to produce the best pen.**

You would be foolish to rush into the market unprepared, especially with Parker's hard-earned reputation for quality at risk. Five years may seem long enough to get all of the bugs out of a new ballpoint-pen design. But what if more time is needed? Pens are more complicated

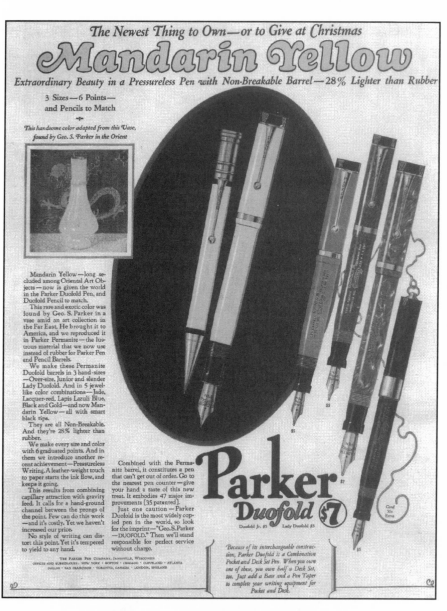

The Newest Thing to Own—or to Give at Christmas

Mandarin Yellow

Extraordinary Beauty in a Pressureless Pen with Non-Breakable Barrel—28% Lighter than Rubber

3 Sizes—6 Points—
and Pencils to Match

*This handsome color adapted from this Vase,
found by Geo. S. Parker in the Orient*

Mandarin Yellow—long se-
cluded among Oriental Art Ob-
jects—now is given the world
in the Parker Duofold Pen, and
Duofold Pencil to match.
This rare and exotic color was
found by Geo. S. Parker in a
vase amid an art collection in
the Far East. He brought it to
America, and we reproduced it
in Parker Permanite—the lus-
trous material that we now use
instead of rubber for Parker Pen
and Pencil Barrels.
We make these Permanite
Duofold barrels in 3 hand-sizes
—Over-size, Junior and slender
Lady Duofold. And in 5 jewel-
like color combinations—Jade,
Lacquer-red, Lapis Lazuli Blue,
Black and Gold—and now Mandarin Yellow—all with smart
black tips.
They are all Non-Breakable.
And they're 28% lighter than
rubber.
We make every size and color
with 6 graduated points. And in
them we introduce another recent achievement—Pressureless
Writing. A feather-weight touch
to paper starts the ink flow, and
keeps it going.
This results from combining
capillary attraction with gravity
feed. It calls for a hand-ground
channel between the prongs of
the point. Few can do this work
—and it's costly. Yet we haven't
increased our price.
No style of writing can dis-
tort this point. Yet it's tempered
to yield to any hand.

Combined with the Perma-
nite barrel, it constitutes a pen
that can't get out of order. Go to
the nearest pen counter—give
your hand a taste of this new
treat. It embodies 47 major improvements [35 patented].
Just one caution — Parker
Duofold is the most widely cop-
ied pen in the world, so look
for the imprint—"Geo.S.Parker
—DUOFOLD." Then we'll stand
responsible for perfect service
without charge.

THE PARKER PEN COMPANY, JANESVILLE, WISCONSIN
OFFICES AND SUBSIDIARIES: NEW YORK · BOSTON · CHICAGO · CLEVELAND · ATLANTA
DALLAS · SAN FRANCISCO · TORONTO, CANADA · LONDON, ENGLAND

Parker
Duofold $7

Duofold Jr. $5   Lady Duofold $5

*Because of its interchangeable construc-
tion, Parker Duofold is a Combination
Pocket and Desk Set Pen. When you own
one of these, you own half a Desk Set,
too. Just add a Base and a Pen Taper
to complete your writing equipment for
Pocket and Desk.*

In its advertising, Parker cited "47 major
improvements" in the manufacture of the Parker
Duofold fountain pen. Thirty-five of these
innovations were awarded patents.

instruments than most people realize. Suppose all of your competitors have stampeded into a new technology that is still decades away from being practical?

Setting a target date for producing a ballpoint pen could easily backfire. Your workers may feel so much pressure to produce a good product that they will cut corners and instead produce something that is not absolutely top of the line.

Do not let your competition make you think that the ballpoint pen is crucial to the survival of the Parker Pen Company. The market for Parker fountain pens is quite different from the market for ballpoint pens. Ballpoint pens are aimed at the everyday consumer. You can find them in discount, five-and-dime, and office supply stores.

Parker fountain pens, however, are works of quality and craftsmanship that people often purchase as gifts for others rather than for their own daily use. A large percentage of your sales occurs just before the holiday season. Instead of the mass-market outlets where ballpoint pens are sold, Parker sells its fountain pens through 12,500 dealers in exclusive jewelry shops and department stores. Therefore, while you should keep your eye on ways to include ballpoint pens in your line of products, you need not worry that those inexpensive ballpoints will hurt your current sales of high-quality fountain pens.

Option 4 **Buy a small company that already produces ballpoint pens.**

The enormous popularity of the ballpoint pen has created a serious dilemma for Parker. The company cannot afford to let the rest of the industry pass it by with

Like this Parker 51, all Parker pens have their highest sales during the holiday season, just before school begins in autumn, and at graduation time.

new technology. Yet Parker cannot afford to risk its solid reputation for excellence in design and manufacture to produce a relatively new and untested product.

But there is a way that Parker can do both. The company can continue to make expensive, high-quality fountain pens. At the same time, it can buy a smaller company that already manufactures a line of ballpoint pens. In this way, Parker can compete for a share of the growing ballpoint-pen market. But because the Parker name would not be on this other pen, people would not associate it directly with Parker, and Parker's reputation would not be damaged should the pen perform badly.

In the meantime, you can begin applying Parker's innovative research and high standards to the ballpoint pen and gradually make improvements on it. Eventually, you should reach a point where you produce a high-quality ballpoint pen that you will be proud to put the Parker name on.

Parker's reputation is so good that you will have no trouble finding one of the more than 250 ballpoint-pen manufacturers to join forces with you in this venture.

YOU ARE THE EXECUTIVE.
WHAT IS YOUR DECISION?

Option 1   Meet the challenge by producing a ballpoint pen immediately.

Option 2   Set a five-year target for producing ballpoint pens.

Option 3   Stay out of the ballpoint-pen business for as long as is necessary to produce the best pen.

Option 4   Buy a small company that already produces ballpoint pens.

Kenneth Parker, son of founder George Parker, refused to enter the ballpoint-pen field before his company could create a pen that would meet Parker's exacting standards of quality.

The Parker Pen Company chose *Option 3*.

Almost 58 years after George Parker founded the company, his son, Kenneth, carried on his obsession with producing the best merchandise on the market. Brushing off the temptation to rake in some quick and easy profits from the public's fascination with ballpoint pens, he instead looked at the big picture. "We are committed to upgrading both ourselves and the industry," Parker said. "We want to stay in business another 58 years."

To Kenneth Parker, ballpoint-pen technology was still in the developing stage. With the existing technology, the Parker Pen Company could not make a ballpoint that met its strict standards. That ended any discussion of following *Option 1* and immediately challenging the competition. The company also found *Option 4* unacceptable because Parker wanted to avoid any connection with lower-priced, lower-quality products. Throughout its history, the Parker Pen Company had made no apologies about charging more for its products because its pens were of higher quality than those of the competition.

Parker also saw no point in setting a timetable for producing a top-quality ballpoint pen. He believed that quality always came first. If the company could develop a great ballpoint pen in five years, fine. But if the company had to spend 50 years before perfecting the pen, it would wait that long.

Kenneth Parker refused to commit Parker to adopting ballpoint-pen technology at all. "If and when Parker brings out a ball-point pen, it won't resemble anything now on the market," he declared.

RESULT

Most of the 250 companies that jumped into the ball-point-pen business earned hefty profits. For example, Eversharp, one of Parker's larger competitors in the old-line fountain-pen business, earned a $2.5-million profit within six months on its "Capillary Action" ballpoint pen. As the ballpoint-pen craze dominated the industry, the Parker Pen Company suffered losses. In the 1950s, *Business Week* magazine wrote that Parker's "leadership has been shaky in recent years."

But after several years of spiraling sales, the ball-point-pen market crashed. The pens simply were not as good as their manufacturers had advertised. Customers found the poor quality of the ink especially troublesome. And the pens' slow-drying ink created an unexpected problem. It allowed forgers to lift a perfect signature by pressing a hand or a sheet of paper on the original and then transferring it to another document, producing a perfect forgery. Eversharp lost more than $3 million because the company had to repair or replace so many of the defective pens that it had guaranteed.

As customers grew disillusioned with their ball-points, manufacturers had to lower their prices to sell their merchandise. New and cheaper pens were being sold for as little as 15¢—down from $15 just a few years earlier. That all-out price war drove many manufacturers out of business, and others barely managed to survive.

By the mid-1950s, those companies that had remained in business improved the quality of their ballpoint pens, so they once again became acceptable.

Paper-Mate had made the greatest advances and captured the bulk of the ballpoint-pen business.

In 1954, Parker finally entered the competition by introducing the Jotter, which had five times the ink capacity of any other ballpoint pen. With the Jotter, Parker gained entry into the ballpoint-pen field with a product that maintained the company's reputation for quality.

More than 3,500,000 Parker Jotters were sold during the pen's first year on the market. Because customers had so much faith in the quality of Parker products, they were willing to pay almost twice as much for a Jotter as for any other ballpoint.

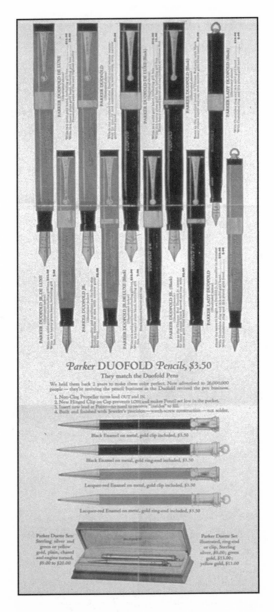

To highlight the quality and durability of the Parker Duofold, the company advertised that the pen still worked after falling 3,000 feet to the ground from an airplane.

ANALYSIS

While Parker stayed out of the competition, its rivals enjoyed tremendous initial success with what was essentially an unpolished gimmick. But Kenneth Parker was eventually proven to be correct in his belief that the ballpoint pen of 1945 was years away from being a satisfactory product.

Standing firm with its old line of fountain pens while rivals were making money from ballpoints required both courage and discipline. It also saved the Parker Pen Company millions of dollars as well as the embarrassment of a tarnished image. As *Newsweek* reported when the demand for ballpoints plunged, "To get out of the swift-moving, razzle-dazzle ball-point pen business still wearing a shirt was a trick few could turn." Unlike most of its competitors, Parker had kept its integrity intact by waiting almost 10 years to introduce a high-quality ballpoint pen.

As smaller pen manufacturers dropped out of the market, Parker eventually found itself facing fewer but larger and stronger competitors. Under those circumstances, it could no longer compete by simply holding on to its share of the high-priced corner of the pen market. Ballpoint pens, after all, were simple and unstylish writing instruments.

Although Parker's top-of-the-line ballpoint cost only about half as much as the company's least expensive fountain pen, Parker recognized that if it wanted to stay in the huge ballpoint-pen market, it would have to sell cheaper pens. The company broadened its sales and preserved its reputation by purchasing Eversharp and making it a division of Parker. Eversharp manufactured lower-priced ballpoint pens under its own label. Meanwhile, with its upper-end ballpoints as well as its high-priced fountain pens, the Parker Pen Company maintained its reputation for top-quality writing instruments.

2

DUPONT
LEATHER LOOK-ALIKE
1963

In the past, your chemical company, DuPont, has hit the jackpot by creating new materials that take the place of natural products. Because your new products have allowed manufacturers to produce so many items quickly and cheaply, you have been able to make a great deal of money from them. Now researchers in your Fabrics and Finishes Department report that they have succeeded in developing a synthetic leather, which they have named "Corfam."

The initial testing on Corfam as a substitute for leather in shoes looks promising. But making Corfam is a complicated and expensive process. What will you do with this new material you have developed?

BACKGROUND

DuPont is one of the oldest and largest businesses in the United States. Dating back to the beginning of the nineteenth century, the company originally manufactured gunpowder. It has since expanded to become one of the world's leading chemical producers, and its research and development efforts have created new materials and products that have changed the world.

The company's most celebrated triumph was the development of nylon. Led by Wallace Carothers, DuPont chemists had experimented with synthetic fibers

Through the years, DuPont has grown from a gunpowder manufacturer to a company with more than 1,200 products that touch all aspects of our lives.

Wallace H. Carothers began a textile revolution when he and other DuPont chemists created a new synthetic fiber that was called nylon.

for a decade before they discovered how to produce this durable plastic. They found that, along with numerous other uses, nylon worked well as an affordable substitute for silk in women's stockings.

The millions spent in refining the process and building plants to produce nylon paid off handsomely for DuPont. From the instant they arrived in stores in May 1940, the inexpensive nylon stockings sold spectacularly well. By 1948, DuPont had built four new factories to keep up with the demand for nylons and was raking in nearly $40 million yearly in sales. For the next two

People waited for hours to buy new and inexpensive stockings made from nylon. On May 15, 1940, the first day they were in the stores, 4 million pairs were sold to eager customers.

decades, DuPont continued to make more money on nylon than on any of its other products.

Ever since DuPont created nylon, its scientists have been searching for another new synthetic product that would match their earlier success. Synthetic leather has been an inviting target. DuPont began research into possible leather substitutes in the 1930s. That effort gained momentum in the 1950s, when marketing experts predicted a shortage of leather in the future.

There was little competition for synthetic leather because the only artificial leather shoes already on the market were made of cheap vinyl-coated fabric. They were stiff and uncomfortable and, worst of all, they did not breathe as leather did. For wearers, this meant suffering unbearably hot feet.

DuPont researchers worked closely with the shoe industry to develop a synthetic leather product from which comfortable shoes could be made. In 1964, after several decades and an investment of roughly $60 million, the researchers finally perfected a sophisticated process to produce Corfam.

Corfam looks and feels similar to leather, but it is much more durable and easier to clean. Best of all, it contains one million pores per square inch, which allows feet to breathe as easily as in leather shoes. The main drawback is that producing Corfam is costly and complex. At the present time, shoes made with Corfam would be as expensive as shoes made of the finest quality leather.

THE DECISION IS YOURS.

As an executive at DuPont, what will you do with the Corfam product?

Option 1 Go full-speed ahead into production.

The situation with Corfam is almost identical to that with nylon a quarter of a century earlier. At that time, products such as silk stockings were expensive because they were in short supply. Thus, nylon filled an enormous consumer demand as a substitute for these scarce products. Corfam will fill a similar large demand for the leather products that are projected to be in short supply in the future.

Market research indicates that the human population is increasing at a rate much faster than that of the cattle from which leather is made. Therefore, it is predicted that by 1983 the demand for leather products will be 30 percent higher than the supply. To take advantage of the growth in demand that is expected, you need only manufacture a product that is superior to anything offered by your competitors.

Right now you have a product that is perfectly suited for the shoe industry, which uses about 85 percent of the available leather. Corfam is vastly superior to the cheap vinyl shoes that are the only leather substitutes on the market. And, in many ways, Corfam is better than leather itself. Corfam matches leather in appearance and texture and in its ability to breathe, but it is lighter and more flexible. Moreover, Corfam is not susceptible to water damage, and, as it does not scuff as easily, it seldom needs polishing.

With all of these advantages, Corfam cannot help but be a success. True, the product is a little on the expensive side, but as your chemists continue to refine their process, the cost of producing the synthetic leather should go down. Even at its present level, Corfam is no more expensive than top-quality leather.

Your research staff has worked hard to give you a fine product that fills an obvious need, so you should move quickly to get the most benefit from their achievement. More than 25 rival companies are trying to create

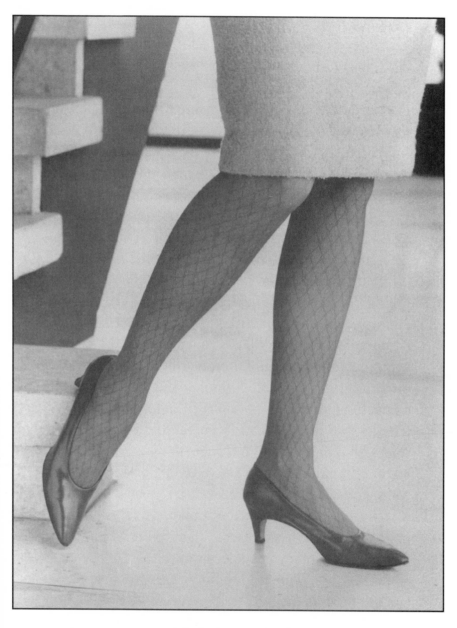

In appearance and feel, the new Corfam shoes rival those made from top-grade leather and keep their new look longer than leather does.

a synthetic leather, and you never know when one of them will come up with a better product than yours—a product that will cut into or capture your sales.

Option 2 **Go into limited production and carefully test market the product.**

Although Corfam looks like a sure winner, you should proceed with caution because the high price of producing Corfam gives you little margin for error. If Corfam does not meet your customers' expectations for a high-quality pair of shoes, the results will be disastrous. Therefore, you had better take your time and begin by carefully testing the public's reaction.

The preliminary reports that you have received about customers' enthusiasm for Corfam shoes are encouraging, but they are not very thorough. New products often fascinate consumers, but these same customers often return to their old brands. Will customers really switch from leather to Corfam and then stay with it? Will they believe that Corfam is as comfortable as leather? And what if problems with Corfam develop months down the line? You should first test market Corfam in a number of cities and towns and provide free samples to people who are on their feet much of the day, such as teachers, police officers, or bank tellers. Then you can see whether Corfam lives up to your expectations.

DuPont has no need to hurry into production with Corfam because the leather shortage is not predicted for 20 years. In the meantime, your process for producing Corfam is so complex that there is little danger of competitors stumbling onto your secret for making it.

Option 3 **Shelve the project.**

No new consumer product is a sure thing. Despite the vast amounts of money that companies spend on research and development, about five out of every six new products fail. Undoubtedly, the creators of these failed products thought as highly of them as you do of Corfam. There are at least three good reasons why Corfam is not going to be DuPont's nylon of the 1960s.

The first reason is the cost factor. Nylon was far cheaper to produce than the silk it replaced. Corfam, however, is as costly to produce as the finest leather. Initially, the price of Corfam shoes will be about the same as top-quality leather shoes. The fact that they are far superior to vinyl shoes means nothing because Corfam will not be competing against vinyl shoes. Those who are interested in cheap synthetic shoes will continue to buy vinyl, and those who can afford expensive shoes may prefer to stay with real top-grain leather. So your only hope of success is to reduce the cost of producing Corfam.

Second, a powerful U.S. industry will no doubt see Corfam as a threat. The silkworm farms that nylon put out of business were in foreign countries, but Corfam would challenge the $700-million-per-year American leather-tanning industry. Leather makers are not going to sit back and let you take their business without a fight. They will probably advertise heavily to convince consumers that leather is better than the synthetic Corfam.

Third, there are always problems whenever you try to expand a small-scale experiment into full-scale production. With a chemical process as complicated as Corfam's, those problems could be more serious than usual.

John Nikolitch (left), pilot plant manager, and sales manager Charles A. Lynch inspect a sheet of Corfam.

Option 4 **Use Corfam as a replacement for leather, but not for shoes.**

You might not want to challenge the tanning industry directly. If the tanners feel threatened, they could fight back with all kinds of negative publicity that could be damaging to your reputation. Yet DuPont cannot afford simply to walk away from a product in which it has already invested $60 million.

A good compromise would be to introduce Corfam as a synthetic alternative to some leather accessories, such as belts, handbags, vests, and jackets. The leather industry may not see this as a major threat and, therefore, probably would not invest much in any attempt to thwart DuPont.

A move toward producing such items would give customers time to get used to your product gradually. Then, when the expected leather shortage begins to occur within the next 20 years, DuPont will be in a perfect position to ease into the production of shoes. Because of the shortage, tanners will be selling all they can produce and yet will be unable to meet the demand. That should make them less fearful of the impact of synthetic leather on their business. Even if they criticize Corfam, the tanners will have less influence over customers who by then will be familiar enough with your product to buy Corfam shoes.

YOU ARE THE EXECUTIVE.
WHAT IS YOUR DECISION?

Option 1   Go full-speed ahead into production.

Option 2   Go into limited production and
              carefully test market the product.

Option 3   Shelve the project.

Option 4   Use Corfam as a replacement for
              leather, but not for shoes.

DuPont chose *Option 2*.

Because of the complexity of the manufacturing process for Corfam, DuPont was confident that competitors would not beat them to the market with a synthetic leather of similar quality. Therefore, company executives decided that they could afford to conduct further tests on a product in which they had already invested so much of their time and money.

To field-test Corfam, DuPont built a small plant in Newburgh, New York. There the company tested 15,000 pairs of shoes on representative wearers, including Newburgh police officers, who spent a great deal of time on their feet.

Corfam performed well in this test market. Those who tried Corfam shoes expressed particular satisfaction with how well the shoes kept their newly polished look with a minimum of care. Only about 1 wearer in 12 had any complaints about discomfort. DuPont's surveys comparing wearers' responses to Corfam, leather, and vinyl shoes found that

3 percent found leather uncomfortable;
8 percent found Corfam uncomfortable;
24 percent found vinyl uncomfortable.

After studying these favorable conclusions, in 1963 DuPont made arrangements to produce Corfam for more than 30 shoe manufacturers. DuPont then went into mass production at Old Hickory, the plant it had bought near Nashville, Tennessee, to manufacture Corfam.

Old Hickory plant manager Karl Ackley (left) and William Lawson, head of the Corfam project, examine a large roll of Corfam before the final stage of production.

RESULT

The new Corfam shoes were an instant success. "Men have been up to their knees in mud and just put them under a faucet or used a sponge" to clean them, marveled one observer. According to a DuPont official, customer acceptance was "even better than we hoped." In fact, demand for the new shoes grew so rapidly that the company could not produce Corfam fast enough to fill all of its orders from the shoe manufacturers.

The glow of success, however, wore off quickly. DuPont wrestled with troublesome technical problems in attempting to adapt the complex process to mass production. Nothing the company tried could reduce the cost of making the material.

In addition, the leather industry doubled its advertising budget and launched an aggressive campaign against synthetic leather. Customers began to complain that Corfam shoes were *too* indestructible—they remained tight after months of wear and never felt broken in. Worst of all, the price of cattle hides dropped 40 percent at just about the same time that Corfam came on the market. That meant that real leather shoes could be made even more cheaply than DuPont had anticipated.

By 1966, DuPont's "Step into the Future" marketing plan had stumbled. Not only did Corfam shoes fail to compete with fine leather, they could not even match the sales of far cheaper vinyl imports from Europe and Japan. Although sales improved between 1968 and 1970, Corfam fell far short of the success that DuPont had predicted for its product.

In March 1971, DuPont gave up trying to cut the costs of Corfam production. Instead, the company announced that it would stop manufacturing the synthetic material and would gradually withdraw Corfam products from the marketplace over the next 12 months.

ANALYSIS

DuPont wisely proceeded with caution on a new product in which it had invested so much time and money. But not even this cautious approach protected the company from blundering with Corfam. A wealth of consumer research is useless if a company cannot interpret the research correctly. Although corporations expect to be slightly off in their projections, they hope that if some polls indicate more consumer acceptance than there will be, other polls will underestimate that acceptance. William Lawson, head of the Corfam project, explained that "with Corfam, all of the errors were on the wrong side, and they were important."

DuPont's researchers had overestimated the product's strengths, and they did not pay enough attention to its faults. Corfam's ability to keep its shape had been touted as a major selling point, but this proved to be a liability when customers complained that their shoes never felt broken in. Market research had shown DuPont that Corfam was probably less comfortable than leather. But instead of focusing on reducing the difference in comfort level between Corfam and leather, the company chose to highlight the fact that Corfam was more comfortable than vinyl.

In addition, DuPont's scientists misjudged their ability to reduce production costs. Because Corfam was so expensive, its competition was against top-quality leather, and, in that contest, Corfam lost. The leather industry helped shovel dirt on the new product's grave by advertising the superiority of leather. "We really overestimated [Corfam's] value-in-use," admitted DuPont executive Edwin Gee. Business analysts estimate that the Corfam mistake cost DuPont as much as $100 million.

3

BOEING
SOARING OR CRASHING
1966

Your company, Boeing, is the largest aircraft manufacturer in the world. Since the process of developing a new commercial airplane consumes many years and millions of dollars, you cannot settle for building whatever products the customers and the commercial airlines seem to prefer today. Instead, you have to plan ahead so that in the future, when the designs you are working on now are ready to fly, they will be exactly what the airline industry needs.

Predicting the requirements of commercial airlines 5 to 10 years in the future is a risky business. Will they want more speed, more passenger room, or some improved version of what you are currently producing? A wrong guess could waste so much time and money that it could cause even a strong company like yours to fail. What plans will you choose for Boeing to pursue?

BACKGROUND

The Boeing Company started out as a hobby for a wealthy businessman. William Boeing, who had made his fortune in the timber business, liked to spend his spare time tinkering with airplanes. He proved to be so good at building them that he and naval officer G. C. Westervelt founded an aircraft-manufacturing company in Seattle, Washington, in 1916.

The Red Barn, shown here in 1917, was the original headquarters and factory of the Boeing Airplane Company.

Company founder William Boeing (right) and Eddie Hubbard, an early Boeing pilot, flew the first North American international airmail route from Victoria, British Columbia, to Seattle, Washington.

Over the years, the Boeing Company developed a solid reputation in its field, especially with the aircraft that it had built for the U.S. government during World War II. Government orders for military aircraft, however, did not provide a steady, dependable source of income, so the company started to build aircraft for the growing passenger airlines.

In 1952, Boeing faced a decision similar to the one you face today. At that time, Boeing executives debated the approval of plans for the 707, America's first commercial jet-powered aircraft. The risks were tremendous. Boeing would have to sink a fortune into planning and developing a replacement to the slower propeller-driven planes. Then, if the 707 did not perform up to expectations or appeal to the commercial-airline companies, the high-flying Boeing Company would fall like a rock.

Boeing president William Allen made the decision to bet the life of the company on the 707. It was a high-stakes gamble. The plane cost so much to develop that 10 years passed before Boeing made its first penny of profit. But the 707 proved to be a gold mine, and Boeing has now sold over 700 of these airplanes. At the ceremony celebrating the 707th 707, one company official declared

The Boeing 707 ushered in a new age of air travel as the United States' first commercial jet liner.

that the sale of 707 airplanes represented "about 500 more than we ever dreamed we could sell." The success of this gamble catapulted Boeing into the position of one of the world's most profitable companies at a time when other aircraft manufacturers were struggling to survive.

But 14 years have passed since Boeing created the 707. In that time, world markets have expanded and international businesses have thrived. The prosperity of the U.S. economy has also made it possible for many more people to afford international travel. All of these changes have dramatically increased demand on the commercial airlines.

Industry experts have formed extremely different visions of the aircraft of the future. Those who believe that speed will be the most important concern of commercial airlines have proposed building supersonic aircraft that can whisk passengers to their destinations at 1,800 miles per hour—about three times as fast as jets currently travel. Many U.S. lawmakers are concerned with staying at the forefront of technology and find this option so attractive that they are willing to spend millions of dollars to help finance the production of such a plane.

Other industry experts believe that airlines will demand much larger planes to serve the growing numbers of passengers. They propose building a plane that is up to three times as large as the 707, which seats fewer than 200 passengers. Still others believe that airlines of the future will be most concerned with convenience and that customers will want a greater choice of flight times. In order to accommodate them, commercial airlines will have to put a larger number of smaller planes in the air.

The Concorde, a joint British and French SST venture, was designed to fly at greater than Mach 2, or twice the speed of sound.

THE DECISION IS YOURS.

As a Boeing Company executive, which aircraft technology will you explore?

Option 1 **Focus your research and development on supersonic airliners.**

Supersonic passenger travel is clearly the wave of the future. The French and British have been pouring money into their 1,800-mile-per-hour supersonic transport (SST) for years and expect to have planes ready for use soon. These aircraft will be able to whisk passengers from the east coast of the United States to Amsterdam or Paris or London in only three hours—more than twice as fast as conventional jets. Furthermore, the United States government is willing to devote $1.5 billion to the project. That is a substantial amount of money, and the more of Boeing's resources you also commit to developing an SST, the quicker you will reap the rewards of its success.

Some industry analysts forecast that commercial airlines throughout the world will purchase at least 500 of these super-fast aircraft at a total cost of $20 billion. As a

Author Robert Serling wrote that President John F. Kennedy had an "obsessive desire" for the United States to remain competitive in all aspects of aerospace technology, including supersonic transport.

leader in the aircraft-manufacturing industry, you cannot afford to concede this huge, profitable market to your European rivals.

Although the price of developing such a speedy passenger aircraft will be staggering, Boeing will probably have to foot the bill for only a fraction of the total cost because the U.S. government will also provide support. Government officials have been casting a nervous eye on the European SST venture. Many of them believe that the government has a vital interest in assuring that the United States at least keeps pace with the technology of other nations. Noting that the European governments have been heavily involved in financing the SST, American lawmakers will be under great pressure to help domestic companies even the odds.

Option 2 Focus your research and development on a jumbo jet.

Just because the Europeans have made the decision to build an SST does not mean the decision is a wise one. The Europeans will come to regret pouring so much of their money into something that is more of a high-priced toy than a true consumer product.

The benefit of cutting off a few hours of flight time is simply not worth the enormous costs involved in developing SST technology because only a small percentage of airline passengers fly the long trips for which supersonic flight would make much of a difference. This means that you would be committing an enormous amount of effort and money to a technology that will do little more than help the rich shave time off of their international flights.

Furthermore, plans for the SST have triggered intense opposition from environmental groups that are concerned about the noise and the possibility that supersonic flight will contribute to the depletion of the ozone layer in the earth's atmosphere. You can expect these groups to fight hard against using taxpayer funds to finance an American-made SST.

Boeing would do well to pay attention to one of its recent market surveys. Your engineers drew up several designs for a new plane and asked airline executives for their reaction. One design seated 250 passengers; another, 300; and a third, 350. The airlines favored the largest of the designs. With more and more people flying each year, the airlines are having trouble meeting the demand for seats. The costs of buying and operating one plane to service 350 passengers would be far less than buying and operating two smaller planes for those same 350 passengers. Thanks to dramatic engine improvements in recent years, building such a large passenger plane is technologically possible.

Option 3 **Focus your research and development on smaller planes.**

The main problem with the SST and the jumbo jet is that engineers will have to design both aircraft from scratch, using new technology. This will cost a staggering amount of money. In either case, Boeing would have to spend billions of dollars before it received any revenue. Under such conditions, the product has to be a huge success or Boeing will go broke. You already have a large, stable, profitable company. Why put that at risk?

Consider also that building huge passenger aircraft could create a problem of inconvenience. Suppose 350 people in Boston want to travel to Chicago on March 15. If an airline company assigns a jumbo jet to carry the passengers, then all of its passengers will have to leave at the same time. But if 100 passengers want to leave at dawn, 100 at noon, and 150 more late at night, many will find it inconvenient to have only one flight time. An airline company flying three smaller planes at three different times would satisfy more customers than one that relied on a single jumbo jet.

For these reasons, Boeing should focus on building smaller passenger aircraft. Such planes would not require innovations in engineering and design and could be developed and built without risking the company's future.

Option 4 Focus your efforts on improving the planes you have now.

The U.S. economy is entering a downturn, so this is not a good time to be considering new aircraft models. Businesses and individuals are always cautious about spending money during uncertain economic times, and developing even a smaller, fairly conventional aircraft would cost a great deal of money. If the economy stays in a rut, you could be introducing expensive new planes at a time when the commercial airlines that usually purchase your product would be reluctant to buy anything.

Instead, this may be a perfect time to sit tight with the models you already have. Some of your American competitors, particularly Lockheed, are struggling to survive. Meanwhile, the Europeans have already committed themselves to the SST, which may prove to be an economic disaster. With your competitors in such sad shape, you should be able to pile up profits and strengthen your position. In five or six years, you will completely dominate the industry and have such huge cash reserves that you will then be able to develop any kind of airplane you want with very little risk.

YOU ARE THE EXECUTIVE.
WHAT IS YOUR DECISION?

Option 1   Focus your research and development on supersonic airliners.

Option 2   Focus your research and development on a jumbo jet.

Option 3   Focus your research and development on smaller planes.

Option 4   Focus your efforts on improving the planes you have now.

*On the day of the 747 rollout Boeing chairman
William Allen (standing), shown here with future
Boeing chairman Thornton Wilson, predicted that
producing the 747 would be a huge success for Boeing
and a giant step forward for the airline industry.*

Boeing chose *Option 2*.

Boeing had reached the top of its field because of its willingness to focus on long-term planning instead of short-term profits. It was not about to go against that tradition by sitting tight with the products that it had.

William Allen, who had taken a chance on the 707, also bore the responsibility for the jumbo-jet decision. According to *Fortune* magazine, Allen's 707 decision was "the first of a series of spectacular gambles that have now become an Allen trademark." In July 1966, Allen lived up to his reputation. He placed the entire company on the line by deciding to develop a jumbo jet even larger than the initial plans—the 490-passenger 747.

Boeing, however, did not abandon its interest in the SST. By pooling its resources with several other investors, it continued to explore the possibility of building such an airplane. But the Seattle-based company had only to make a relatively small commitment because the federal government financed nearly 90 percent of the research that Boeing conducted on the SST.

RESULT

Initially, Boeing appeared to have taken a dangerous and unnecessary risk. Less than a year after the company committed its resources to the 747, the federal government awarded Boeing a huge contract to build the SST. President Richard Nixon's administration supported the supersonic-aircraft project, and legislative leaders such as Gerald Ford (who would succeed Nixon as president) confidently predicted that Congress would approve $1.5 billion in funding. With that kind of government support, the SST appeared certain to be the aircraft of the future.

In the meantime, the 747 ran into snags. Design changes and problems with locating parts delayed production and increased the cost of development to about double what Boeing had anticipated. The first 747s finally rolled out of the factories in 1969, but they "could not have been introduced at a worse time," stated *Business Week* magazine. Most commercial-airline companies were

The 747 plant at Everett, Washington, is the largest industrial facility in the world. Forty football fields could fit under the building's roof.

in serious financial trouble and did not have the money to place any orders for new aircraft.

Boeing's profits plunged by 88 percent that year, and sales of 747s ground to a halt. The company went 17 months without a single domestic order for the new airplane. To make matters worse, the commercial airlines surprised Boeing by changing their flight schedules. Instead of moving to mass flights between several major U.S. cities, many airlines began providing more frequent flights between a larger number of cities.

Because they had committed their resources to the jumbo jet, Boeing could not compete in the growing market for new, smaller planes. Falling on hard times, the company had to lay off about one-third of its 101,500 Seattle-based employees between 1968 and 1970. The aircraft builder's decision to concentrate on the 747 seemed so poor that *Fortune* magazine asked, "Has the era of Boeing domination of the commercial jet-aircraft industry ended?"

But the predictors of doom had spoken too soon. In 1970, events turned with startling speed in the 747's favor. Growing opposition to the SST from economists and environmentalists led to increasing pressure on the government to kill the project. On March 24, 1971, the U.S. Senate voted 51 to 46 to end government funding of the SST.

At the same time, commercial airlines were attracted by figures that showed the jumbo jet offered the lowest operating costs of any aircraft on the market. They began to order 747s, and in 1970 Boeing filled orders for customers from 42 countries.

The Boeing 747, the world's largest jetliner, measures 235 feet in length, weighs 350 tons, and can carry 490 passengers.

The 747 soon recouped its high cost of development—and more. By the end of the 1970s, more than 400 of Boeing's 747s dotted the skies. The Seattle company not only sold every 747 it manufactured, but it also had a three-year waiting list for the jumbo jets. In 1979, the 747 was largely responsible for Boeing's triumph as the most profitable of the 500 largest corporations in the United States.

Meanwhile, the European SST proved to be the financial disaster that its critics had predicted, and it survived only with continued subsidies from the European governments to make up for its unprofitability.

ANALYSIS

William Allen understood the risk he was taking, and he was none too comfortable with it. The jumbo-jet project came very close to destroying Boeing. Allen later confessed that the 747 "was really too large a project for us. We undertook it because we felt that we had no other alternative if we continued to head to commercial business" and no longer depended on military contracts.

William Allen had been a lawyer for Boeing for 20 years before being appointed company president in 1945. Known as a man of spotless integrity, he successfully defended Boeing's projects before Congress.

Allen's decision required a great deal of courage. "People called us crazy for predicting we'd sell so many," said Thornton Wilson, Boeing's chairman of the board. But Boeing's tradition of looking ahead and taking calculated risks made the commitment possible. The decision to build the 747 paid off so well that today it ranks as one of the best decisions in U.S. corporate history. As business writer Jeremy Main described Boeing's success in 1992, "On a scale virtually unmatched by any other U.S. corporation, it dominates its world market and is the nation's largest exporter."

In holding back on the SST, Boeing avoided a potentially deadly trap. According to Allen, the SST posed "the most difficult design problem we've ever faced." Boeing concluded it was not willing to gamble that the benefits of the SST would be worth the enormous cost of its development.

As long as the federal government paid most of the bills, Boeing had gone along with a U.S. research program into supersonic airliners. Using the government's money was a wise decision because, as *Forbes* magazine noted, "a heavy commitment to a supersonic transport program would have crimped the company's ability" to develop profitable products. Nothing in the history of the European SST hints that Boeing would have made money off the venture. Because this Seattle company exercised caution, it was able to walk away from the supersonic project without serious damage after the U.S. Senate had pulled the government out of the venture.

4

SONY

VCR STATIC

1974

Your electronics company has been pushing to develop a new product with tremendous sales potential—the videocassette recorder (VCR). You now have a workable design for a VCR that will be both affordable and small enough for consumers to use in their homes.

In order to develop this technology, you and some of your competitors have been sharing research. These companies do not have a product ready for the market. But since they know virtually everything that you know, they cannot be far behind. How do you take advantage of your new technology and your head start to get the most benefit from your new product?

Sony was established by Masuru Ibuka and Aiko Morita in a bombed-out department store in postwar Tokyo, Japan. A year later, the company moved to its current site, shown here.

BACKGROUND

Since the 1950s, Sony—originally Tokyo Telecommunications Engineering Company and renamed for *sonus*, the Latin word for "sound"—has been a leader in pioneering electronic products for consumers. It has forged breakthroughs in the manufacture of transistor radios and television picture tubes.

The quest for an affordable videocassette recorder for the home began in 1954, when American engineers built the first magnetic-tape machine capable of recording images as well as sound. Sony was one of many companies that began making videotape machines. These large, expensive machines were used primarily by television stations, which no longer had to rely on live broadcasts for all of their programming.

Over the next 15 years, electronics companies sought ways to produce smaller, less expensive videocassette-recording machines. Sony formed an agreement to share technology in this area with Matsushita (which marketed products under the brand names Quasar and Panasonic) and JVC (a small independent company owned by Matsushita). This agreement would save all three companies time and money in their efforts to produce a video recorder for home use.

In keeping with this agreement, you have offered to license your new videocassette recorder to these other companies. They, however, have declined the offer. In fact, they are moving forward with plans to develop their own products that operate under different formats. To add insult to injury, they have offered to license their products to you.

This poses a potential danger to all three companies. Videocassette recorders will create a market for videocassette products, such as movies, how-to programs, and exercise tapes. If each of the three companies comes out with its own VCR format designed to work in a slightly different way, then cassette producers will face a problem. Because the cassettes they manufacture and sell will work

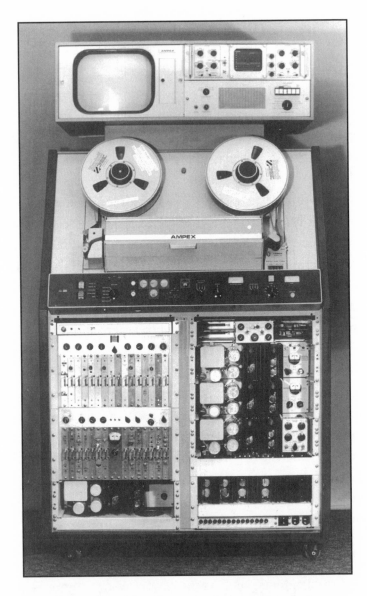

The Ampex machine that recorded sound and pictures revolutionized television broadcasting by allowing networks to prerecord programs. Almost as soon as it was built, engineers began to explore ways to develop a smaller and more affordable unit for home use.

with only one of the three formats, consumers who own videocassette recorders with one of the other two formats will not buy these cassettes.

On the other hand, if cassette producers make cassettes to fit all three formats, they will be forking out three times as much money without gaining any more customers for their product than if all VCRs used the same format. In addition, people will likely be confused about which format to buy and irritated that they have to search for products compatible with their VCRs.

There is also another factor to consider. Cassette manufacturers will probably choose to make cassettes geared to the most popular of the three formats because this decision will bring them the most sales at the lowest cost. Customers will then buy the most popular format of VCR because it will allow them to use the best selection of products. This cycle will feed on itself until the most popular product becomes the industry standard and leaves the other formats without any buyers.

THE DECISION IS YOURS.

As an executive at Sony, how will you proceed with the new VCR technology?

Option 1 **Move cautiously and conduct consumer research before introducing your product. Then share your technology with your competitors.**

The stakes are high because the pressure for the industry to adopt one VCR format will be tremendous. Whichever format becomes the standard will succeed spectacularly. Those that lose will fail utterly. You might as well be the worst for all the good second-best will do you in this market.

The VCR format that the most consumers purchase will become the industry standard. So the question you need to answer is "What will cause consumers to purchase my VCRs instead of those produced by my rivals?" The answer is the product's practicality and availability.

Sony was already world famous for creating consumer electronics products, such as this reel-to-reel tape player, that had a reputation for excellence.

Practicality is the most important element. Being first to introduce a new product means nothing if your rival comes out with something that customers like better. So far your company has done little consumer research to determine what people want in a VCR, and you had better find out. Sure, your machine may be a technological wonder, but consumers are not interested in a machine that can do tricks. They want a machine they can use.

Once you are certain that your product is the best, you must make it available to the public. You want to fill the marketplace with your VCR because the format that is on the most store shelves has the best chance of outselling the others. Once you reach a clear advantage in sales, the industry will have little choice but to adopt your format as the standard.

For this reason, you must share your format with as many competitors as possible, including U.S. companies, and make the marketing of your product as easy as possible for these competitors. If you share the technology and use generous terms when you give your competitors licensing rights—such as letting them put their own company name on the VCRs—you may sacrifice money and prestige in the short run, but you will win the all-important race to become the industry standard.

Option 2 **Move quickly with the product you have and guard your technology.**
There are only so many ways to build a videocassette recorder. Thus, there will be little significant difference between your product and the product your competitors try to sell. Even if others make a slight improvement in

quality, the name of the game is speed. That lesson should be obvious after seeing the experience of JVC, one of your competitors.

In the battles for commercial videotape machines that would be used for broadcasting, JVC actually had developed a videotape process that was slightly better than anyone else's. But by the time it was ready to go to market, a competing system already had been established as the video standard. JVC never got a foothold, and it failed in its efforts to market a videotape machine that used its superior process.

You have perhaps a two-year head start over your competitors. That is an enormous advantage. If you hit the market fast enough and hard enough, you can establish your own VCR format as the industry standard before your competitors have released theirs.

You would be foolish to waste that lead by doing consumer research. Sony has always put out first-rate products, and your highly respected engineers have worked hard to create the best VCR possible. If you start overanalyzing the situation in an attempt to satisfy everyone, you will end up pleasing no one. Besides, this is an entirely new product. How can customers tell you what they want in a product that has never existed before?

Once your format wins acceptance as the industry standard, you would be wise to take maximum advantage of that achievement by making sure the Sony name is on as many VCR units as possible. Name visibility will help the public and your competition to recognize your role as the industry leader. Dealers and consumers will respect your proven ability to build and market marvelous new devices, and they will be eager to try other new products that you introduce in the future.

JVC and Matsushita have actually done you a favor by declining to license your format. Take advantage of this by licensing your product only to those companies that will agree to put the Sony name on their machines. By moving quickly, you can win acceptance of your VCR format as the industry standard without help from anyone else.

Option 3 **Move quickly with the product you have and share your technology.**

For the reasons stated above, you must have confidence in your product and boldly move to take advantage of your lead over your competitors.

But you do not want to squander your advantage by keeping tight control over your format. Your most important job is to get your format accepted as the industry standard, and nothing should stand in the way of that goal. The best way to guarantee this acceptance is to make your format as widely available as possible. Therefore, you should work out deals with as many electronics companies as you can, including firms in the United States, to let them sell machines using your format under their company names.

Option 4 **Adopt the JVC format.**

You do not want to get into a costly battle with competitors, each of whom is desperate to establish its own format as the industry standard. You could prevent that by entering into a licensing agreement with JVC to produce machines that use their format. That move would instantly establish one standard format.

Of course, JVC could just as easily agree to enter into a licensing agreement using *your* format, but the company has already declined to do this. Now you have to ask why a small company such as JVC would accept the risk of challenging your format as the industry standard. Two basic differences exist between their machines and yours: your videocassettes are smaller, and your videocassettes record fewer minutes.

What if consumers decide that having longer playing-time is a more important feature than compact size?

Sony VCRs had compact tapes (right) with a one-hour playing time, while the JVC format had a larger tape that could play for two hours.

Perhaps JVC has done some consumer research and knows something that you do not. If so, *Option 4* would be the safest approach. True, it would give you no advantage over your competitors, and it might hurt your pride, but at least you would not get burned. Once a standard format is established in the industry, you can figure out other ways to beat your competitors.

YOU ARE THE EXECUTIVE. WHAT IS YOUR DECISION?

Option 1   Move cautiously and conduct consumer research before introducing your product. Then share your technology with your competitors.

Option 2   Move quickly with the product you have and guard your technology.

Option 3   Move quickly with the product you have and share your technology.

Option 4   Adopt the JVC format.

The Morita family had a long tradition in Japan's alcoholic beverage business as producers of a popular brand of sake. But eldest son Aiko Morita (shown here), who had been groomed to take over the family business, instead turned his efforts toward consumer electronics and cofounded the Sony corporation with his partner, Masuru Ibuka.

Sony chose *Option 2.*

Sony had confidence that its engineers had designed and built the best VCR product, which it called "Betamax." The company was especially pleased with its success in being able to store so much visual information on such a small cassette.

The Japanese company also took pride in its reputation as a pioneer in its field. According to Masuru Ibuka, one of the company's top executives, "The key to success for Sony . . . is never to follow the others." This view ruled out *Option 4.*

In addition, Ibuka believed that consumers could not properly understand a product that had never existed

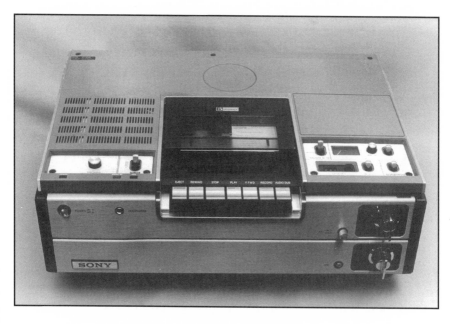

The Sony Betamax was first sold in Japan in 1975.

before. Therefore, taking the time to conduct a detailed survey of customers' likes and dislikes about this revolutionary new product would be a waste of time. This line of reasoning ruled out *Option 1*.

Sony believed that if it moved forward quickly with its product, it could gain control of a huge new market before any rivals could offer a challenge. Everyone else would have to adopt Sony's format. Sony's head start put it in a position of great strength, and the company decided to take advantage of this. It arranged deals with only those electronics companies that would market machines with the Sony format and use the Sony name.

RESULT

The Sony Betamax VCRs arrived in stores across the United States late in 1975. Demand for the product, however, was not as great as Sony had hoped. Despite having no competitors, the company and its few partners sold fewer than 200,000 units in 18 months.

JVC took longer to unveil its Video Home System (VHS) product because it tailored its product to a list of features that it believed the public would want in a VCR. Then JVC worked to sign on major electronics companies, such as RCA, Magnavox, and General Electric, to market the VHS format it had created.

JVC also sought the advice of electronics companies that had considerable experience in the introduction of new products to U.S. consumers—the product's largest potential market. One of RCA's suggestions was to set the price at $995, which was lower than the $1,100 that Sony

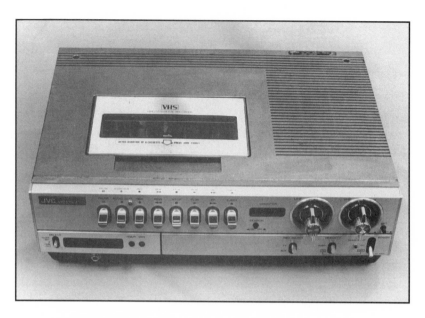

Introduced almost two years after the Betamax, JVC's VHS videocassette recorder quickly caught the attention of consumers and soon became the industry standard.

was charging. Although this move cut deeply into JVC profits, keeping the price under $1,000 was necessary in order to entice consumers to buy the JVC product.

The VHS-format machines designed by JVC arrived on the U.S. market in August 1977. Customers liked the fact that the machine could record two hours of television programming instead of the one hour that Betamax recorded. This meant a VHS machine could record an entire TV movie while Betamax could not.

Because of their longer recording time, wider distribution, and lower price, the VHS machines quickly outsold Sony's Betamax. Companies that produced and sold or rented videotapes saw this trend and concentrated their efforts on making products compatible with VHS. This, in turn, increased the demand for VHS players and reduced the demand for Betamax.

Sony tried to fight back and regain its market share by making improvements to its machine and by allowing more companies to use its format. But it was too late. Sony's rivals had also kept improving their machines, and, as a result, Sony could not climb out of the hole it had dug for itself.

By 1980, VHS was outselling Betamax by a two-to-one margin, and it climbed to a three-to-one lead by 1982. Refusing to admit defeat, Sony continued to push its Betamax machines. By the end of 1985, however, VHS held a commanding 80 percent of the VCR market. The Betamax was doomed.

Sony continued to hold out hope for its Betamax until 1988. Then, with its share of the booming VCR market in the U.S. shriveled to less than three percent, Sony finally accepted VHS as the industry standard and began manufacturing VCRs with the VHS format.

ANALYSIS

Being first is not always as important as having the right product. Sony could not take advantage of being first to the marketplace because consumers far preferred its competitor's product.

Sony's engineers had enjoyed great success with making products that were smaller and more convenient than those of their competitors. In keeping with this tradition, they focused on how to make the videotape cassette as small as possible, only to find that consumers were not particularly interested in the size of the cassette.

On the other hand, JVC had looked at the problem from the consumer's point of view. Instead of asking what might be technologically possible, this company's engineers had asked themselves what people would want. The researchers decided that recording and playing-times—features that Sony had disregarded—would be the key concerns of potential customers.

Sony's rush to be first to the marketplace may have contributed to its oversight. According to Shizuo Takano, leader of the videocassette-recorder team at JVC, "Sony was working faster than we were, which might explain why they didn't examine more closely the issue of whether the cassette should play for one hour or two." Sony had further erred in too strictly controlling its format. By insisting that the Sony brand name be on virtually every machine that it licensed for sale, Sony lost valuable allies in the industry. This resulted in limiting the availability of its machines to consumers.

JVC, however, saw that the licensing of its VHS technology was critical for its success. The more distributors that sold its technology, the better the chances that the VHS format would become the industry standard. Even if JVC helped its competitors by sharing its technology, it would still reap the benefits of a thriving new industry. "The market is large enough to hold everybody," commented Takano. "One single company does not have to monopolize the whole profit."

Sony's rivals also listened to the advice of experienced U.S. marketers who said that JVC should sacrifice a little profit to get the VCR price low enough to tempt U.S. consumers to buy the new product.

Because of its commitment to a compact cassette—which, in hindsight, was not an important feature to consumers—Sony failed to sell enough machines to establish the Betamax as the industry standard. The slow sales gave Sony's rivals the opening they needed, and they took advantage of it. Sony then aggravated its mistake by waiting too long to correct its error. The company's stubborn failure to abandon the Betamax until the bitter end reduced Sony to a minor player in the VCR business that the company had helped to create.

5

JOHNSON & JOHNSON
THE POISONED PILL
1982

You are in charge of one of the world's leading suppliers of health-care products. One of your most popular products is Tylenol, an over-the-counter pain reliever that comes in capsule form. In September 1982, you received the shocking news that some demented person had tampered with packages of this pain reliever. Police officials believe that poisoned capsules of your product are responsible for at least seven deaths in the Chicago area.

Obviously, consumers want nothing to do with a product that could kill them. And you want to do all you can to avoid more deaths. What will you do with this product that is now causing a national panic?

BACKGROUND

Johnson & Johnson has been one of America's most trusted companies ever since Robert, James, and Edward Johnson began their partnership in New Brunswick, New Jersey, in 1885. Beginning by producing surgical dressing on the fourth floor of a wallpaper factory, the three brothers built their business into a nationally recognized firm on a solid foundation of honesty, fairness, and quality.

The company's over-the-counter pain reliever is one of its most successful products. Johnson & Johnson, however, does not directly manufacture this product. It owns a smaller company, McNeil Consumer Products, that produces and packages the pain reliever in both tablet and capsule form. Johnson & Johnson then markets the

Left to right: Robert, James, and Edward Johnson started their company by manufacturing and packaging sterile bandages.

From its humble beginnings in this warehouse in the 1880s, Johnson & Johnson has grown into a world-class corporation.

product under the brand name Tylenol. Tylenol, which is extraordinarily popular, has captured 35 percent of the market and outsells its four closest competitors combined.

The recent events have rocked the once unshakable position of Johnson & Johnson's pain reliever. Now people associate Tylenol with poisoning. As soon as criminal investigators determined that poisoned capsules of Tylenol had caused the Chicago deaths, they set out to discover how the capsules had become contaminated. By coincidence, the first two bottles of poisoned capsules came from the McNeil plant in Fort Washington, Pennsylvania. Working with the police, the FBI looked into operations at the McNeil factories, but they found no evidence of tampering there. A third bottle of tainted capsules came from the McNeil plant in Round Rock, Texas. This suggested that the bottles had been tampered with after they had left the factory. Therefore, the manufacturer was not at fault.

Within a week of the first death, police concluded that someone had taken packages of the pain reliever from half a dozen supermarkets and pharmacies in the Chicago area. This person then opened the bottles, took apart the capsules that held the powdered medication, and filled them with deadly cyanide. Afterward, the person put the capsules back together, resealed the caps on the bottles, and returned them to the same stores from which they had been taken.

Investigators have no leads on this terrible crime. Meanwhile, Johnson & Johnson has received a letter from an unknown person who warns that more people will die unless the company sends $1 million. Police officials in other cities are reporting cases of capsule tampering by copycats. You have no way of knowing how many more packages of your pain reliever contain cyanide.

The public is in a panic, and consumers are concerned about the medicines in their cabinets. If Tylenol can be tampered with, why not other products? They are especially leery of Tylenol, however. Sales of the pain reliever have dropped off rapidly and are likely to plunge even further.

THE DECISION IS YOURS.

As a Johnson & Johnson executive, how will you handle this crisis?

Option 1 Leave Tylenol on the market and gradually develop and phase in new tamper-resistant packaging.

This may seem like a risky thing to do in view of the fact that there may still be some poisoned pills on store shelves. But both FBI director William Webster and Food and Drug Administration commissioner Arthur Hayes urge you to take this course of action. Although they realize there is some risk of additional deaths if you leave the product on the shelves, they are more concerned

Prior to the Tylenol scare, the new FBI director, William Webster, had enjoyed a distinguished career as a judge on the U.S. Court of Appeals.

with the signal you will send to potential terrorists if you pull your product from retail stores. If terrorists see that lethal product tampering can force a giant corporation like Johnson & Johnson to take on the enormous expense of recalling 22 million packages of a product, they may decide to launch widespread attacks against other U.S. industries.

So why go to the horrendous expense of recalling packages when even law-enforcement officials urge you to stand firm? Since 1885, Johnson & Johnson has built a solid reputation for honesty and fair dealing. Eventually, the high regard that consumers have for your company will pay off, and the public's concern about your brand of pain reliever will pass.

People still trust your company. In fact, they probably sympathize with your dilemma and realize that none of this is your fault. The extortion demand provides ample evidence that you are the victim, and the American public will bend over backwards to be fair to you. They will understand that this poisoning was the work of an isolated "nut case" and will soon go back to buying your pain reliever.

Option 2 **Withdraw Tylenol from the market at your own expense and replace it with a new brand name packaged in a tamper-resistant container.**

The success of Johnson & Johnson was built on the principle of integrity. Earlier in this century Robert Wood Johnson, the son of one of the founders, listed the company's priorities in all its dealings. According to Johnson, the company was responsible to four groups of

Robert Wood Johnson, son of Robert Johnson, led Johnson & Johnson from 1932 until his death in 1968.

people in the following order of importance: its customers, its employees, the community where it is located, and its stockholders.

In other words, the company's first job is to look after the interests of the customers who have placed their trust in its products. At this moment, there are capsules marketed by your company that could kill people. Johnson & Johnson's first order of business is to protect the safety of its customers, so it must withdraw all Tylenol capsules from the shelves, regardless of the amount of money this option will cost the company.

Then you must face the fact that, unfair as it may seem, Tylenol has already lost the public's trust. The tamperings have been the focus of unrelenting media attention since they were first reported. Thousands of stories have appeared in the newspapers, and national and local television and radio programs have devoted hundreds of hours of coverage to the killings. More than 90 percent of the U.S. population is aware that your product was involved in the cyanide deaths. This is an incredible amount of publicity, and none of it is good. As a result, consumers are panicked and they will no longer buy Tylenol products.

Although withdrawal and replacement of the product will cost you millions of dollars, the loss will be even worse if you continue to market a product that the public is afraid to purchase.

Option 3 **Withdraw Tylenol and replace it with a new brand name but let McNeil Consumer Products bear the costs.**

For reasons stated above, your Extra-Strength Tylenol pain reliever is doomed, and it must be replaced. But there is a way to cut the huge losses this will inflict on Johnson & Johnson and, at the same time, insulate the company from negative publicity. Johnson & Johnson did not actually produce the deadly pain-reliever capsules. Instead, Extra-Strength Tylenol is manufactured by McNeil Consumer Products, a small independent company that Johnson & Johnson owns. Technically, McNeil, not Johnson & Johnson, should bear responsibility for the capsules and should assume the cost of withdrawing the product from the market.

This course of action would be disastrous to McNeil, which would certainly go out of business. Since Johnson & Johnson owns McNeil Consumer Products, it would ultimately feel the shock of the small company's failure. But because hardly any consumers associate the McNeil name with Johnson & Johnson, letting McNeil take the blame would keep Johnson & Johnson away from any damaging publicity and would give it a better chance of regaining customers with a new product.

Option 4 **Withdraw Tylenol but bring it back on the market with new, tamper-resistant packaging.**

Look back at Robert Wood Johnson's priorities. Customer safety comes first, so you must withdraw the product from the shelves. Employees come second, so you should consider the effect of making the McNeil factories take responsibility. You are responsible to the McNeil workers who have been manufacturing your product. The tragic deaths were not their fault any more than they were the fault of Johnson & Johnson. By allowing McNeil workers to take the blame and responsibility, you would put their factories out of business and good workers out of their jobs.

Making McNeil take responsibility will not insulate Johnson & Johnson. No matter what you do, consumers will associate the murders with your pain reliever. Even if blaming McNeil would keep you more profitable, profits come last on the list of company priorities. This argues against sacrificing people's jobs in order to protect your image and save money.

Furthermore, you do not need to shelter Johnson & Johnson from publicity about this incident. If you accept the cost of removing Tylenol from the shelves to protect your customers, the public will see Johnson & Johnson as a company with integrity that puts the concerns of the customer first. And because consumers trust you, they will be sympathetic to your position once the initial panic is over.

You have spent a great deal of effort and money establishing Tylenol as the leading over-the-counter pain

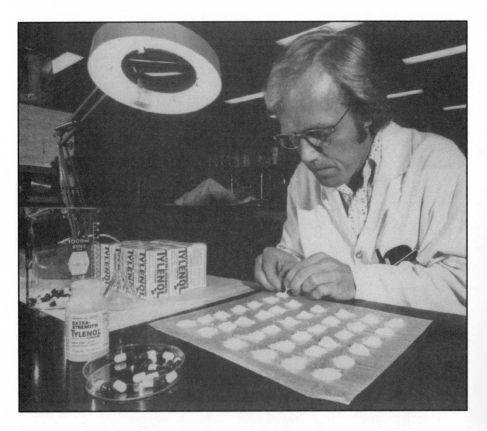

Widespread fear of poisoning has led to the inspection of thousands of capsules. This scientist has already examined over 4,000 capsules, looking for discoloration that would indicate the presence of cyanide in the normally fluffy white medication.

reliever in the country. Customers are shying away from it because of fears about tampering, not because of any dissatisfaction with the quality. To win back their business, you simply need to regain their trust by developing a tamper-resistant package that will reassure them that your product is again safe to use.

YOU ARE THE EXECUTIVE.
WHAT IS YOUR DECISION?

Option 1   Leave Tylenol on the market and gradually develop and phase in new tamper-resistant packaging.

Option 2   Withdraw Tylenol from the market at your own expense and replace it with a new brand name packaged in a tamper-resistant container.

Option 3   Withdraw Tylenol and replace it with a new brand name but let McNeil Consumer Products bear the costs.

Option 4   Withdraw Tylenol but bring it back on the market with new, tamper-resistant packaging.

James Burke, CEO at Johnson & Johnson during the Tylenol crisis, had a greater stake in the product than others because he had been the man behind the creation of that non-aspirin pain reliever.

Johnson & Johnson chose *Option 4*.

Following Johnson & Johnson's guidelines, the company officials repeatedly emphasized that as far as they were concerned, "the health and welfare of the community was the only issue." They took action quickly. On October 5, 1982, the company withdrew all Extra-Strength Tylenol pain-reliever capsules from store shelves. Then, on October 12, Johnson & Johnson took out full-page ads in newspapers throughout the United States, offering customers free Tylenol tablets in exchange for their Tylenol capsules.

Johnson & Johnson's current headquarters in New Brunswick, New Jersey. Following the Tylenol scare, the company formulated a plan for dealing with crises, and executives were given two copies of emergency numbers and names—one for their office and one for their bedside table.

Continuing to follow company priorities, Johnson & Johnson declined to blame the problem on McNeil. According to author Steven Fink, the company went out of its way to embrace McNeil employees. Johnson & Johnson not only absorbed the entire cost of removing the product, but it even found jobs for McNeil workers who were temporarily laid off by the halt in production of Tylenol capsules.

Finally, the company's top executives remained convinced that the public still trusted the Tylenol name. Believing that they could count on the public's sympathy and sense of fair play, they stayed with the Tylenol brand. On November 11, 1982, five weeks after the recall, company officials announced the return of Tylenol in new, tripled-sealed packaging. Their aggressive advertising campaign to win back customers scared off by the Tylenol poisoning included distributing coupons worth $2.50 toward the purchase of any Tylenol product.

RESULT

The cost of the recall of Extra-Strength Tylenol was nearly $100 million, enough to shake the stability of even a corporation as large as Johnson & Johnson. But the recall also recovered two unused poisoned packages, so it may have saved at least two lives.

Johnson & Johnson initially lost customers to other brands of pain relievers, but it quickly won them back. By 1986, Extra-Strength Tylenol had captured 98 percent of the market share that it had held before the capsules had been laced with cyanide.

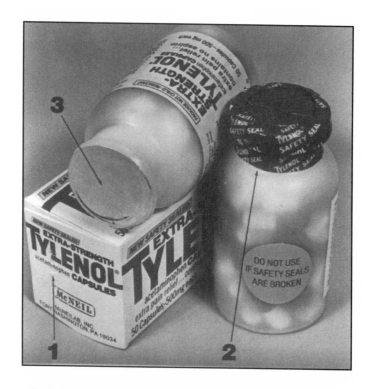

Only five weeks after it was withdrawn, Johnson & Johnson reissued Tylenol with new tamper-resistant packaging. The new package had (1) glued flaps on the box, (2) a tight plastic neck seal, and (3) a strong foil seal over the opening of the bottle.

ANALYSIS

Business analysts are unanimous in their evaluation of Johnson & Johnson's management of the Tylenol crisis as an outstanding example of corporate leadership. In his book, *Crisis Management*, Steven Fink stated that the company performed so well that its image actually improved after the horrible events. According to Fink, "Johnson and Johnson emerged from the Tylenol crisis a better company, or at least a better-*perceived* company."

JOHNSON & JOHNSON
PARENT OF
McNEIL LABORATORIES

GENTLEMEN;

AS YOU CAN SEE, IT IS EASY TO PLACE CYANIDE (BOTH POTASSIUM & SODIUM)
INTO CAPSULES SITTING ON STORE SHELVES. AND SINCE THE CYANIDE IS INSIDE
THE GELATIN, IT IS EASY TO GET BUYERS TO SWALLOW THE BITTER PILL.
ANOTHER ~~BEAUTY~~ BEAUTY IS THAT CYANIDE OPERATES QUICKLY. IT TAKES
SO VERY LITTLE. AND THERE WILL BE NO TIME TO TAKE COUNTER MEASURES

IF YOU DON'T MIND THE PUBLICITY OF THESE LITTLE CAPSULES, THEN
DO NOTHING. SO FAR, I HAVE SPENT LESS THAN FIFTY DOLLARS.
AND IT TAKES ME LESS THAN 10-MINUTES PER BOTTLE.

IF YOU WANT TO STOP THE KILLING THEN WIRE $1,000,000.00 TO
BANK ACCOUNT #84-49-597. AT CONTINENTAL ILLINOIS BANK CHICAGO, ILL
84-49-597.

DON'T ATTEMPT TO INVOLVE THE FBI OR LOCAL CHICAGO AUTHORITIES
WITH THIS LETTER. A COUPLE OF PHONE CALLS BY ME WILL UNDO
ANYTHING YOU CAN POSSIBLY DO.

*A short time after the cyanide deaths, James Lewis
sent this letter to Johnson & Johnson. Lewis used the
bank account number of his wife's former employer in
the letter, seeking revenge for a bounced paycheck.
Convicted of attempted extortion for this act, James
Lewis spent more than 12 years in jail.*

When asked to explain their success in dealing with the crisis, Johnson & Johnson executive Larry Foster repeatedly stressed that "the company acted responsibly and it acted fast." He added, "We earned [the public's] loyalty by treating them honestly and fairly." The company did this by putting the consumer's interests first. It assumed a huge financial loss and probably saved lives in the process. By shouldering the entire cost of the recall,

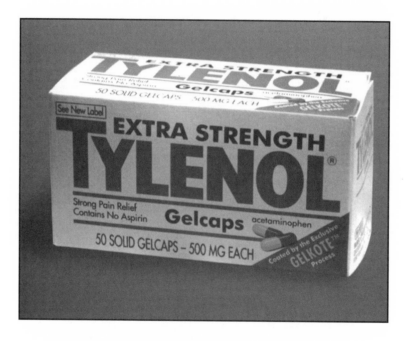

Johnson & Johnson faced a number of copycat crimes until April 1984, when Extra-Strength Tylenol capsules were finally discontinued and replaced with capsule-shaped tablets called caplets. The gelcaps pictured here, introduced in July 1988, combine the qualities of the capsule and the caplet because they are easy to swallow and have a tamper-resistant solid core.

Johnson & Johnson also earned the respect and loyalty of the McNeil workers, who would have lost their jobs if McNeil had gone out of business. The company gambled that the public would see Johnson & Johnson as the innocent victim of a psychopath. That is exactly what occurred. As a result, the company easily won back the business of its former customers—and no doubt gained some new customers as well.

6

OSBORNE COMPUTERS
GROWING PAINS
1982

Your Osborne Computer Corporation can proudly boast that it is one of the fastest growing companies in U.S. history. You opened for business less than two years ago and your sales already approach $100 million per year, with projections of reaching $300 million in 1983.

The problem with such astounding success is that it sometimes seems that you have attracted as many competitors as customers. Many rival companies are now introducing personal computers aimed at tapping into the booming market you have discovered. What will you do to fight off their challenge?

BACKGROUND

In 1981, Adam Osborne, who had made his fortune by writing books that explained computers to the nonexpert, founded the Osborne Computer Corporation. At that time, most computers had far more complex programs than people needed or wanted, and the machines were not packaged in a format that people found convenient to use in the office or at home. Instead, computer companies had primarily targeted large businesses, public institutions, and scientific laboratories. Osborne believed that the computer industry was making a huge mistake by designing products for only computer experts.

Giant computers like these Control Data CYBER computers were standard before Osborne's revolutionary small business computer made computers available to a larger market.

Osborne saw what he called "a truck-sized hole" in the computer market for a small, portable, affordable computer. He believed that many small-business owners, secretaries, and others who needed help organizing information would appreciate the timesaving advantages of a computer if it was affordable and easy to use. These everyday needs were being neglected by the large computer companies.

Realizing that the first company to fill this gap in the market would make millions, Osborne quickly organized a company that combined a computer monitor, a disk drive, and a keyboard in a portable computer package. This product, called the Osborne 1, was the first portable business computer.

Most industry experts scoffed at Osborne's business plan because they did not believe anyone could sell a high-quality, portable computer for the $1,795 price of the Osborne 1. But Osborne's company came up with ingenious ways to keep the price hundreds of dollars less than its competitors' without sacrificing profit. First, the company made no attempt to manufacture all of the parts for the Osborne 1. Instead, Osborne built its computers from standard industry components. Then the company signed a deal with the Computerland chain of stores to market and sell its computers.

Second, Osborne cleverly arranged special deals with software suppliers. In exchange for bargain prices on software, Osborne offered the suppliers shares of company stock. As a result, the company was able to include with its computers a software package free of charge—a $1,500 value!

The Osborne 1 was the first easily portable personal computer. Small enough to fit under the seat of an airplane, it was an instant hit with business travelers.

This deal—a computer and free software—saved the customer not only money but also the trouble and anxiety of finding useful, compatible software. "We made the purchasing decision convenient by bundling hardware and needed software in one price," explained Osborne.

Customers eagerly snapped up the Osborne 1 from this new, unknown company. Osborne shipped its first machine in July 1981. Six months later, it had sold 8,000 computers. In 1982, sales skyrocketed to 110,000 units. By the end of that year, Osborne's work force had increased from 141 to more than 600.

Osborne grew even faster than the legendary Apple Computer Company. In fact, within 18 months, it was on the verge of joining such established firms as Apple, IBM, Commodore, and Radio Shack as one of the computer industry's five leading computer manufacturers. The bottom line was that Osborne sold its computers for far less than any rival while still earning twice as much profit per machine as the industry average.

But now other companies have seen how well one company can do by manufacturing small, portable, mass-market computers. Consequently, they want to grab a share of that booming market. More than 300 companies, including the gigantic IBM corporation, are now working feverishly to introduce their own small computers by copying Osborne's cost-cutting methods.

THE DECISION IS YOURS.

As an executive of the Osborne Computer Corporation, how will you hold on to your extraordinary success?

Option 1 **Stay with your product and keep prices low.**

An old adage says, "Dance with the one who brought you to the ball." In business terms, this means to go with the strategy that has brought you success. For Osborne, the key to success has been keeping the cost of its computer low.

Adam Osborne is convinced that the computer industry is so enthusiastic about developing new features in computers that it has "lost its drive to push prices down." For computer experts, the joy and challenge of their craft is in finding exciting new ways to use computer technology. But these new features also add to the price of the computer.

Although there is not much glamour in making plain machines that have only modest capabilities, you have found that simple machines are what the vast majority of customers want and can afford. Your company also happens to have a talent for finding creative ways to trim costs. You should keep taking advantage of that ability and continue to give customers a basic machine at the lowest possible price.

Option 2 **Proceed cautiously, hold back on production, and sink your profits into developing a variety of computers.**

The nature of economic competition will quickly put an end to your impressive business success. You have achieved huge sales and profits because you tapped into an unrecognized computer need as well as a manufacturing strategy that no one else was using at that time. But now competitors have taken note of your success and are making products aimed at the market that once belonged exclusively to you.

Soon there will be so many competitors fighting for the same customers that many companies will not survive the competition. One computer industry analyst has observed that "the most vulnerable firms are the smaller firms that specialize in a particular segment of the market." That description fits Osborne. Despite Osborne's phenomenal growth, it is tiny compared to IBM or Apple, and it has specialized in only one segment of the computer market—lightweight, inexpensive computers.

Firms that grow at a dizzying rate often forget about planning for the future. Osborne can no longer keep pouring all of its money into cranking out more of the same machines, even though there still appears to be a great demand for them. If your competitors come out with a better and less expensive product, your company will be stuck with a warehouse full of machines that no one wants.

In order to survive the next phase of competition, you will need to expand your product line. Your tremendous sales and earnings over the past 18 months have given you the time and the finances to do that.

Option 3 Start producing IBM-compatible computers.

Osborne's astounding success came about strictly because you realized that middle-income people wanted low-priced personal computers. You simply began producing an affordable computer before anyone else could. But that is now history. Because the rest of the industry is now wise to savvy strategies, you are about to lose your advantage.

One competitor plans to introduce a computer that is six pounds lighter than your Osborne 1, and many other companies are developing products with quality equal to or better than the Osborne, but at a lower price. Most of them will be marketing computers with a much larger monitor than the Osborne 1's cramped five-inch screen.

*Computer giant IBM began producing smaller
personal computers to cash in on the market that
Osborne had discovered. Believing that IBM systems
would dominate the market, other companies tailored
their computers to run programs similar to IBM's.*

In addition, Japanese competitors are rushing into
the computer market, and the Japanese are masters at
cutting costs and reducing prices in electronics. You may
not be able to match the quality and the price of their
machines. Thus, you may lose your hold on the low-
priced market for computers.

If Osborne tries to establish itself as a leader in other areas of the computer industry, IBM can outspend the company 100 to 1 on research, development, marketing, and production. So rather than gloat over your success, you would be wise to acknowledge that you do not have the resources or the expertise to become dominant in the computer industry. Instead, you should be thankful that you made the money you did and accept IBM as the big power in the business. Settle for creating machines that can run IBM programs.

Option 4 Crank out the Osborne 1 quickly before its market dries up. Develop new, improved products and announce the innovations while you are developing them.

The Osborne 1 will soon be obsolete. The tiny display screen that kept the price so low was acceptable to consumers when there was no affordable choice. But it now looks terribly primitive compared to the larger screens of your competition's new low-cost machines. Furthermore, other companies will soon be selling computers with the capability for color graphics, which the Osborne 1 lacks. Despite these problems, sales will continue to be strong until competitors get their products established in the market. Therefore, keep producing the Osborne 1 but, at the same time, move quickly on new products. The computer industry is changing at a breakneck pace, and any machine that is now state of the art will be obsolete next year.

In a field that changes so quickly, a company that is able to spot trends and recognize how best to adapt any new technology to the needs of consumers will stay ahead of the competition. Osborne's success was not a one-time fluke. The company has shown a remarkable ability to identify consumer needs, and it can continue to do so. Although your competitors' new products are already stealing attention away from Osborne, if you keep your company's name in front of your customers, you will let them know that you are still an innovative force in the industry. Hold consumers' attention and respect by letting them know about the innovations you are developing for your new models. Then get those new models into production as quickly as possible.

YOU ARE THE EXECUTIVE.
WHAT IS YOUR DECISION?

Option 1   **Stay with your product and keep prices low.**

Option 2   **Proceed cautiously, hold back on production, and sink your profits into developing a variety of computers.**

Option 3   **Start producing IBM-compatible computers.**

Option 4   **Crank out the Osborne 1 quickly before its market dries up. Develop new, improved products and announce the innovations while you are developing them.**

Adam Osborne, founder of Osborne Computer Corporation, was known for his showmanship when introducing new computer developments.

Osborne chose *Option 4*.

"I am not much of a diplomat," Adam Osborne admitted. "I make enemies." It was not in his nature to concede the computer field to his competitors, IBM, or the Japanese.

Osborne had dreams of building his company into a $1-billion giant within two years. That kind of growth called for an aggressive marketing strategy. The company chose to spend heavily on ads for its Osborne 1 and to keep that computer in full production.

At the same time, Osborne prepared to branch out with three new products: the Vixen, the Executive 1, and the Executive 2. The company planned to sell the Vixen at a cheaper price than the Osborne 1, and thereby re-establish Osborne as the company of choice for those seeking the least expensive computer. The more advanced Executive 1, due to be ready for sale in spring 1983, and the Executive 2, due out late that summer, would also give Osborne a foothold in the higher-priced market.

RESULT

Adam Osborne confidently predicted that his company would continue its explosive growth in 1983 and increase its annual sales volume to $300 million. Instead, the Osborne Computer Corporation completely collapsed.

The Osborne 1's small screen was a greater problem than the company had guessed. By the beginning of 1983, the first wave of more than 60 competing models hit the

Adam Osborne with the Osborne Executive 1. The introduction of the Executive, a more advanced version of the Osborne 1, unexpectedly caused sales of the Osborne 1 to drop dramatically.

market. They immediately raised customers' expectations for the features that a computer should have. Osborne soon lost customers to newer, larger-screened models. And when IBM made an unexpectedly aggressive bid to capture control of the portable computer market, Osborne could not compete. In April, Adam Osborne received stunning news from his auditors. That year, his company would probably lose $8 million.

The Osborne Computer Corporation tried to recover sales by giving consumers a preview of its new Executive 1, a machine with more of the features that customers were demanding. Then it scrapped its plans for the Vixen, a computer that now appeared to be too primitive to appeal to consumers. The company then promised that the Executive 2 would be compatible with the products of the new market king—IBM.

The Executive 1, however, was not ready to be shipped until May. By that time, sales of the Osborne 1 had stopped. Although the company desperately struggled to recover, it could not escape from the mountain of debt it had accumulated. Osborne trimmed its work force and only 80 employees remained by September 9, 1983. Five days later, unable to pay $5 million in overdue bills, the company filed for bankruptcy.

ANALYSIS

Adam Osborne had shown expert skill in starting a new business, but he had no experience or training in managing a business that had grown to a considerable size. The company's astounding early success had created some unrealistic goals and expectations. Convinced that his company would continue its rapid growth, Osborne had projected sales of $1 billion in 1984. But he failed to anticipate the fierce competition that his initial success would attract or the rapidity with which trends in the computer industry could change.

While Osborne had developed a unique product that appealed to a large number of consumers, it did not remain unique for long. Even at the peak of Osborne's success, the Osborne 1 was rapidly growing obsolete. Its small screen, which had been acceptable to customers a

Adam Osborne's concept of the small computer remains with us today. Modern portable computers, like this IBM laptop, are compact enough to fit in a briefcase or knapsack but have more power than the pioneering Osborne 1.

year before, suddenly looked unappealing once consumers saw the competitions' larger screens.

The Osborne Computer Corporation tried to fight back, but it no longer had any advantage over its many competitors. Whatever strategy it tried, such as further price-slashing, could be easily matched or exceeded by its competitors, especially by IBM. As an industry analyst noted, Osborne (as well as about 150 other small manufacturers) was "developing products that do not have a unique feature or competitive advantage."

Although Osborne dropped to a middle-of-the-pack company in a fiercely competitive business, it continued to view itself as an industry leader. Because of its unrealistic self-image, its executives were slow in recognizing IBM's advantage in the market, and the company did not adopt IBM-compatible features until after many of its competitors had already done so.

In its overeagerness to regain the ground that it had lost to its competitors, Osborne then made a fatal error. According to a business analyst, "The foolish announcement of the new Executive computer before it was even ready to go to market practically killed sales for the older Osborne 1." After learning that a vastly superior Executive was on the way, no customer wanted to buy an Osborne 1. In fact, many stores canceled their previous orders. Having been lulled into a false sense of security by its booming sales and lured by a dream of building a billion-dollar company, the Osborne Computer Corporation had spent most of its earnings on expansion. Thus, it did not have the cash to survive a month of no sales and soon went out of business.

7

HARLEY-DAVIDSON
RIDING INTO THE SUNSET?
1982

The future has never looked bleaker at the Harley-Davidson Motor Company. Although your motorcycles command incredible loyalty from serious American bikers, your company is teetering on the brink of disaster. Years of careless management and shoddy quality have finally taken their toll on the Harley-Davidson reputation. Japanese competitors, whose motorcycles are now far superior in quality to yours and are also less expensive, have overwhelmed Harley-Davidson in the U.S. market.

At most, you have a couple of years to keep Harley-Davidson from going out of business. How can your company be rescued?

Winning early motorcycle races and endurance contests helped establish Harley-Davidson's reputation for quality and excellence.

BACKGROUND

Your company traces its roots back to 1903, when William Harley and the three Davidson brothers—Walter, Arthur, and William—assembled their first motorcycle in Milwaukee, Wisconsin. Building large, high-powered, high-quality motorcycles allowed Harley-Davidson to survive in a tough business.

Until the 1960s, your company was the lone survivor among the more than 150 motorcycle companies that had once operated in the United States. Harley-Davidson easily fended off foreign competitors and sold about 70 percent of all motorcycles purchased in the United States.

Nobody in the company was concerned when Honda, a Japanese motorcycle company, decided to challenge Harley-Davidson on its home turf in 1959. Harley motorcycles inspired fierce, almost fanatical, loyalty among American bikers, and those who took pride in revving up their big, rumbling machines scoffed at the idea of buying the smaller, quieter Japanese models.

Although Honda sold only 167 motorcycles in its first year on the U.S. market, the company dramatically changed the American motorcycle business. While Harley-Davidson tended to attract hard-core bikers, Honda appealed to the average consumer. Its inexpensive machines provided economical and enjoyable transportation. Honda soon uncovered a large group of customers who wanted to try motorcycling but did not care for the superheavyweight bike scene. Within a few years, Honda was outselling Harley in the United States.

Fortunately for Harley-Davidson, Honda helped increase interest in all types of motorcycles, so the U.S. company still found itself swamped with more orders than it could fill. By expanding production, company managers tried to take advantage of this booming demand. But in their rush to produce more machines, Harley managers began to cut corners on quality.

The gap in sales and quality between Honda (and other Japanese manufacturers) and Harley-Davidson grew

Honda's 1962 advertising campaign, "You Meet the Nicest People on a Honda," gave motorcycles a new image. Many who previously had not thought of using a motorcycle as transportation now considered buying one.

wider every year. By 1977, the once-proud Harley-Davidson had fallen far behind its Japanese competitors and sold only 5.7 percent of the motorcycles purchased in the United States. Other Japanese manufacturers, such as Yamaha and Kawasaki, had also jumped into the American market to take sales away from both Harley-Davidson and Honda. Honda even pulled far ahead in the super-heavyweight class of bikes that Harley-Davidson had always dominated. Harley's 75 percent market share in the superheavyweight category in 1973 had dwindled to 30.8 percent by 1980.

In an attempt to save their company and their jobs, a group of Harley-Davidson managers bought the struggling company in 1981 after its previous owners had given up on it. When they evaluated the company a year later, even these long-time employees were surprised at what they found. According to Vaughn Beals, one of the new owners, "At first we found it hard to believe we could be that bad—but we were."

The new owners learned, for example, that about 50 to 60 percent of the Harleys that came off the assembly line failed to pass inspection and needed repairs or new parts before Harley-Davidson could send them out to dealers. In contrast, only 5 percent of the motorcycles that came off Honda's production lines required further work. Something was very wrong.

THE DECISION IS YOURS.

As an executive at Harley-Davidson, how will you make your company competitive again?

Option 1 **Overhaul your products and your image.**

Harley-Davidson's problems have come about because the company became lazy and careless during years of ruling the American motorcycle market. It had focused on the image of the roaring, high-powered, highway-cruising bike because it had considered the power, the noise, and the rough ride to be a vital part of the Harley experience. But these characteristics had turned off a great number of potential customers. Many people who might have been interested in motorcycles wanted nothing to do with Harley's scruffy image.

Until Honda arrived, these potential customers had few options in the U.S. motorcycle market. The Japanese companies aimed their products and advertising at this vast, untapped pool of customers—average, middle-class people who were looking for economical transportation and youths who wanted good, clean fun. The Japanese found that many people who would not spend money for huge, expensive Harleys were willing to shell out a few hundred dollars for a smaller Japanese bike.

Harley-Davidson cannot turn its fortunes around unless it broadens its consumer base. You need to get away from the black-leather-jacket image and start producing smaller, less expensive motorcycles that will appeal to a wider range of consumers.

Option 2 **Get tough with quality control on your assembly lines.**

The problem is not that you are making the wrong motorcycles. Twice in the past—in 1925 and again in 1949—Harley-Davidson had experimented with smaller models, but the public had shown little interest in those bikes. And almost none of the other companies that have tried to compete with the small bikes sold by Japanese companies, such as some British manufacturers in the early 1960s, are still in business.

Over the past 10 years, Japanese companies have made far better motorcycles than Harley-Davidson has, and they have been able to sell them for less. Under these circumstances, your company should have folded long ago. In fact, Harley-Davidson's image as the king of superheavyweight bikes is about the only thing the company has going for it right now, and a core group of Americans has bought into the Harley-Davidson mystique. They believe the big, rumbling Harleys are the only motorcycles any true biker would buy. As one bank executive commented, Harley-Davidson motorcycles are "the only product I'd ever seen that people had tattooed on their bodies." For these serious bikers, Harleys are the true American motorcycle.

Customer loyalty was so strong that even when Harley-Davidson was plagued with problems, riders, like the thousands who gather each summer at the Sturgis, South Dakota, motorcycle rally, stayed with the brand.

Your problem is not what you are making, but how you are making it. Harley-Davidson cannot survive if you keep building shoddy motorcycles. You also have to lower your prices, and you cannot afford to spend hundreds of dollars repairing motorcycles that are faulty when they come off the assembly line. If you can come close to the Japanese bikes in quality and price, your legendary status among bikers should be enough to keep you going.

The best way to improve your quality and to reduce expensive repair costs is to get back to the basics that have made U.S. companies leaders in business worldwide. American businesses have traditionally relied on quality-control inspectors to maintain high production standards. You need to hire no-nonsense supervisors who will keep a close eye on your motorcycles through every stage of production.

To motivate assembly-line workers to do a better job, these supervisors can give rewards for good work and penalties for poor production. Harley-Davidson made some similar quality-control efforts in the 1970s. Although these efforts produced positive results, they never brought about the major changes you require. That experience shows that you cannot go at this halfheartedly. Instead, you need to hire a large group of tough inspectors who will pressure employees until they produce a better machine.

Option 3 **Involve your employees in making decisions.**
The traditional method of having supervisors crack the whip over assembly-line workers does not work. And a system that relies on quality-control inspectors is

expensive because it does not discover problems and flaws until after the mistakes have been made. Furthermore, Harley-Davidson has already tried this approach and has never gotten dramatic results with it. You would be foolish to explain away that failure by saying your inspectors simply needed to be tougher.

A far better solution would be to imitate the methods of your Japanese competitors. Honda's factories are neater in appearance and are managed more efficiently than yours. Yet the company employs fewer managers. On a tour of a Honda plant, you saw that relations between the workers and management were more friendly than they are at Harley-Davidson.

Obviously, the key to Honda's success is not the tighter supervision of its workers. In fact, the Japanese follow the principles of employee involvement that were developed by an American consultant, W. Edwards Deming. He believed that leadership in achieving quality should come from the people directly responsible for making the product—the workers on the assembly line.

Deming pointed out that American companies usually rely on upper-level managers to make key decisions. These managers then must do two things to implement the changes. First, they have to convince the workers that the decision was wise. Then they must train the workers to carry out the decision. If a decision proves to be flawed, employees gripe about it and about the incompetency of management, and management cannot alter the decision without looking foolish.

Companies would be better off, Deming believed, if managers first discussed a proposed change with all of

The business management principles of American consultant W. Edwards Deming (1900-1993), who was then nearly unknown in the United States, were a major factor in the revitalization of Japanese industry after World War II.

the workers whom the change would affect. The consultant recommended this tactic because he believed that workers directly involved in a decision might be able to offer valuable insights into the problem. Management could then make important adjustments before making any major changes.

To maintain product quality, Deming insisted that companies needed to train their employees to evaluate their own work. He stressed that people are more likely to take pride in their work if they are given responsibility for its quality and if they have a say in how their plant is run. In fact, they will likely discover problems earlier than the quality inspectors do and will correct them sooner. That is because independent inspectors have to go through three drawn-out steps. First, they must recognize the problem. Then they need to find a solution. Finally, they have to retrain the employee.

Some critics have claimed that this style of management works for the Japanese only because their culture is different from American culture. But Honda is experiencing the same good results with American workers in its plants in the United States.

Option 4 **Ask the U.S. government for help.**

None of the other options will save your company. *Option 1*—trying to change your product line—would alienate your best customers. Following *Option 2*—hiring tough quality-control inspectors—would produce only limited results. And *Option 3*—getting employees more involved—would take time. American manufacturers have not accepted Deming's methods, and workers and management at Harley-Davidson have been at odds for years. As a result, both sides will be very suspicious about your motives when you ask for their cooperation.

In the meantime, Harley-Davidson has too many severe problems to survive on its own. Business analysts say the Japanese motorcycle companies are so far ahead in quality and price that they could put Harley-Davidson out of business whenever they wished. As the final insult,

Honda is now beating Harley-Davidson at its own game. It is producing a better superheavyweight bike at just over half the cost of a Harley and has passed Harley-Davidson in sales in that category.

As if that were not bad enough, Harley-Davidson is also in poor financial shape. Its new owners are not wealthy. They had to go deeply into debt to buy out the company, and there is little cash left for developing new products. Finally, this is not the best of times for many businesses, including motorcycles. Sales have trailed off for all companies because interest rates have climbed so high that customers are thinking twice about taking out a loan to make large purchases.

Given the tremendous odds against you, your survival depends on the U.S. government. Just a few years ago, Chrysler executives saved their auto-manufacturing company from certain failure by asking the government for help. The auto company got the assistance it needed in the form of government backing for loans that helped a nearly bankrupt company transform its product and make an astounding comeback.

You should devote all of your energy to following the same procedure. Remind lawmakers that Harley-Davidson is an American company that employs thousands of American workers. Convince the members of Congress to protect American businesses that are struggling because of foreign competition.

This is a risky strategy. Many lawmakers believe businesses should compete in a free market without any government interference or aid. They supported Chrysler only grudgingly, fearing that if they helped the auto manufacturer, other American companies would line up with their hands out, asking for government help. If you request assistance from the government, it might turn you down as it did when you asked for support in 1978. If aid is refused, you will have wasted a lot of time and effort and done nothing to help your company.

YOU ARE THE EXECUTIVE. WHAT IS YOUR DECISION?

Option 1   Overhaul your products and your image.

Option 2   Get tough with quality control on your assembly lines.

Option 3   Involve your employees in making decisions.

Option 4   Ask the U.S. government for help.

Harley-Davidson chose *Option 3*.

Ever since Harley-Davidson began losing the motorcycle market to Honda, it had blamed its problems on outside factors. The company had claimed everything from cheap labor and dirty business practices to cultural differences had given Japanese competitors an unfair advantage in producing motorcycles.

Company officials did successfully lobby the federal government to raise tariffs temporarily on Japanese heavy-weight bikes, but they did not expect the government to bail them out as it had Chrysler. The company, after all, was in its present predicament because of its own mistakes, and many Americans would resent the idea of using U.S. government money to reward Harley-Davidson for the company's poor performance. "We do not intend to prohibit the Japanese from competing in the American market," asserted new co-owner Vaughn Beals. "Nor are we asking for any kind of financial support from our government."

When the new management compared its factories to Honda's, they saw that the most glaring difference was how the Japanese company managed its plants. According to Harley-Davidson's Ron Hutchinson, management had for years been in charge of quality at Harley-Davidson, and "we had motorcycles that were not as good as they should have been." Honda had far greater employee involvement, and they produced better machines at a lower cost. Harley-Davidson's management concluded that the only way it could compete with Japanese companies was to adopt Honda's methods.

Before he was hired as an executive by Harley-Davidson, Vaughn Beals had never ridden a motorcycle. Six years later, his loyalty to the Harley vision prompted him to plan and direct the 1981 buyout of the company.

RESULT

Changes in Harley-Davidson's management style did not come quickly or easily. Even though the company revamped its assembly-line system to get employees more involved, it continued to lose money. In 1982, Harley-Davidson needed additional bank loans just to keep out of bankruptcy.

In 1983 and 1984, the company did earn more money than it spent, but that seemed too little, too late. Harley struggled to get out from under the weight of the crushing debts it had built up during the bad years. To top it off, Citicorp, Harley's principal lender, decided to get out of the motorcycle industry before tariffs on Japanese bikes expired in 1988. The bank refused to continue providing the overadvances (loans in excess of the lending formula) that Harley depended on, and Harley-Davidson was again threatened with bankruptcy.

Following this narrow brush with failure, Harley-Davidson rebounded with a vengeance. Relations with the unions that represented Harley employees improved dramatically, and workers were made responsible for maintaining the efficiency of the assembly line and the quality of the motorcycles they produced.

Within five years, Harley-Davidson had regained its reputation, its sales, and its stability. In 1983, Honda's superheavyweight motorcycles—Harley's specialty—had outsold Harley-Davidson's by almost two to one. By 1988, Harley-Davidson had turned that around and captured 46.5 percent of the superheavyweight market while Honda controlled just over 24 percent. Harley-Davidson

Harley-Davidson motorcycle riders tend to be rugged individualists who enjoy the spirit of freedom associated with the machine. Each year, thousands of Harley enthusiasts gather in Sturgis to celebrate the Harley experience.

sales continued to grow and, in 1994, it controlled 60 percent of the highly competitive market for superheavyweight bikes. The newly revamped company not only sold every bike it built, but it also had a waiting list of customers who wanted to purchase a Harley.

ANALYSIS

Rich Teerlink, the chief executive officer at Harley-Davidson, observed that waiting around for the United States' and Japanese governments to make a deal that would protect U.S. business interests would have been self-defeating. Harley-Davidson's main problem was that its competitors were managing their businesses far better than Harley was. Whatever else happened, the company had to address that problem in order to survive.

Teerlink gave a large portion of the credit for the company's turnaround to the switch in management styles. Harley-Davidson succeeded in creating an "environment in which an employee feels free to challenge the system to achieve success."

Vaughn Beals, the former manager who had become a part owner of Harley-Davidson, agreed. He pointed out that under the old system, mistakes often occurred when engineers decided on a course of action. The line workers would shake their heads, grumble about the idiots in management, and "wouldn't have lifted a finger to help."

Under the new system, however, managers listened to the assembly-line workers. Acting on their cost-saving suggestions, management initiated scores of improvements that may not have occurred to them. In addition, workers took more pride and interest in their work. Once the company got its house in order, it was able to take advantage of its customer loyalty and regain its position as the king of the superheavyweight bikes.

8

COCA-COLA
THE COLA CONFLICT
1985

Your Coca-Cola beverage has dominated the soft-drink market for decades, and it remains atop the $50-billion-per-year industry. But over the past 10 years, your main competitor, Pepsi-Cola, has been steadily soaking up your sales. If the trend continues, your company may soon lose its number-one ranking.

Recently, while Coca-Cola chemists were developing flavors for the new Diet Coke, they stumbled upon a formula they feel may help you turn the tables on Pepsi. Your taste-panel experts prefer this new formula to the old Coca-Cola recipe.

How will you use this information to defend your company from the Pepsi challenge?

BACKGROUND

Coca-Cola was created nearly 100 years ago in Atlanta, Georgia. An efficient bottling network and steady advertising helped the product to quickly develop a large and enthusiastic following. The flowing Coca-Cola cursive script and its red and white colors are instantly recognizable throughout the world, and advertising experts call Coke the most successful product in history.

Over the years, Coca-Cola's success has attracted dozens of competitors, each with similar cola products. Many of these competitors disappeared from the scene almost as quickly as they arrived. But, for 84 years, rival

Because Coca-Cola inspired many imitators, the company's advertising urged customers to insist on the genuine article. In later ads, Coca-Cola would be known as "the Real Thing."

Pepsi-Cola has been waging a fierce campaign to catch up with Coca-Cola in sales and popularity.

In the 1950s, Coca-Cola held a two-to-one advantage in sales over Pepsi-Cola. But recently Pepsi has been targeting younger customers in its advertising, believing that by dominating that market it will gain customers for life. During the past 10 years, the competitor's efforts have been paying off. Pepsi won a clear-cut victory with an advertising campaign called "the Pepsi Challenge." The company invited people in shopping malls across the country to take blind taste-tests comparing the two colas. The tests convinced many consumers that they preferred the Pepsi taste over Coca-Cola.

Pepsi now outsells Coke in American supermarkets, and the only reason you lead in total sales is due to restaurant and vending-machine business. A large share of these sales is guaranteed in corporate contracts, including one with the huge McDonald's fast-food chain to sell only Coca-Cola products. But if you continue to lose ground to Pepsi-Cola, you could lose those accounts in a hurry.

Your market research indicates that Pepsi's success is due in part to a cola formula that is slightly sweeter and less biting than the Coke formula. The new recipe that your researchers have devised is tailored to this national preference for a sweeter taste.

THE DECISION IS YOURS.

As an executive at Coca-Cola, what will you do with the new cola formula?

Option 1 **Replace the old Coca-Cola product with a heavily advertised new and improved Coca-Cola.**

The figures do not lie. Pepsi is overtaking Coca-Cola, especially in the youth market. Although older customers still prefer Coke's taste, they are also more concerned about their weight and other health issues than young people are. Thus, these older customers are switching to diet brands and alternative drinks. If young people are the mainstay of the popular cola market and Pepsi has the youth market in hand, the Coca-Cola Company may be in big trouble. You need to do something to win back young consumers.

Test marketing shows that the new formula your chemists have created could be just the thing to lure Pepsi drinkers back to Coke. In nearly 200,000 blind taste-tests, the new formula clearly beat both the old Coke and Pepsi.

Some people resist change and may be upset about losing a product that has been part of American culture for nearly a century. But the highly competitive soft-drink market is no place for wallowing in memories of the good old days. You must act decisively and deal Pepsi a blow it is not expecting.

In recent years, your company has benefited from this type of aggressive action. A few years ago, many experts warned against putting the Coke name on any other product. In the long history of the company, no one had dared meddle with the respected name of Coke because Coca-Cola stood for one product only. Why risk cheapening Coke's image by sticking the long-revered name on a new product that might fail?

But Coca-Cola chief executive officer Roberto Goizueta ignored those warnings and, in 1982, introduced Diet Coke. In just three years, Diet Coke has become the leading diet soft drink in the United States and third in sales among soft drinks overall. Such aggressive actions have revived the Coca-Cola Company, which had grown sluggish by living off its past. More bold actions are now needed to fight off Pepsi. Reformulating the recipe for Coca-Cola is, perhaps, the boldest move you can make.

Coca-Cola chairman Roberto Goizueta broke with the tradition of Coca-Cola standing for only one product. Under his leadership, the company put the Coke name on other soft drinks, including Diet Coke and Caffeine-Free Coke. Coca-Cola also bought Columbia Pictures, became active in the television industry, and explored a wide range of other business opportunities.

Option 2 **Keep the old Coca-Cola as your only regular cola product.**

Coca-Cola is such a unique product that ordinary market research does not work for it. While the words "new and improved" may attract consumers to many modern products, they cannot be applied to Coke. In the twentieth century, Coca-Cola has never been new.

The image of an unchanging formula is a great part of the cola's appeal. In selling a product, image is as important as taste, and consumers view Coca-Cola as a product untarnished by cold, impersonal marketing decisions or by modern factory shortcuts. Instead, it is part of American culture and stands as a symbol of good, old-fashioned American values. In a world that changes at a frightening pace, Coke remains constant. It could be dangerous to tamper with a product that is revered by so many people.

To stress this feature, you have advertised Coca-Cola as "the Real Thing." Imagine the mockery you invite if you change the formula so that the real thing is no longer "the Real Thing."

Furthermore, if you replace Coke with a beverage that is more like Pepsi, what happens to the customers who prefer Coke? No one would be selling the product that Coke drinkers now prefer. What if Pepsi were to offer something similar to your old Coca-Cola? Imagine the humiliation of surrendering one of the world's most famous products to your biggest competitor!

In the final analysis, Coca-Cola is still the world's best-selling soft drink. Remember the common saying: "If it ain't broke, don't fix it."

Serving trays, such as this one featuring a Norman
Rockwell painting, as well as calenders, dishes, playing
cards, and countless other paraphernalia and
collectibles have displayed the Coca-Cola trademark
for more than a century.

Option 3 **Keep the old Coke and bring out the new formula under a new name.**

You are faced with two conflicting facts. First, Coca-Cola's "Real Thing" image is too valuable to disturb, and, second, you can't keep losing customers to Pepsi. Also, customers resent being told what they should drink. If you pull old Coca-Cola from the shelves and replace it with a new cola product, you will rob loyal Coke drinkers of their favorite beverage. Motorcycle manufacturer Harley-Davidson learned that customers who are attached to a familiar product will be hostile to alternatives to that product. In other words, don't eliminate the old until consumers have accepted its replacement.

Your advertising agency and most of the executives at Coca-Cola advise you to pursue this option, which will give you the best of both worlds. On the one hand, you don't want to lose the old Coca-Cola's history, unique taste, and long record as the world's leading soft drink. But neither can you afford to sit back and watch Pepsi get a tighter grip on the youth market. The answer is to keep producing original Coke for its loyal fans while introducing the new cola to lure away those who prefer Pepsi's sweeter taste.

This solution is an extension of a policy that has worked well for Coca-Cola in recent years. For most of its history, the company had resisted the idea of expanding its line of products. But in an attempt to appeal to many different tastes, Coca-Cola has begun manufacturing a variety of soft drinks and now produces a lemon-lime drink called Sprite as well as Diet Coke and Caffeine-Free Coke. Plans are under way to introduce Cherry

Coke in the near future. The company could extend this line of products to also include the new cola.

This strategy would put Pepsi on the defensive. If you replace old Coke with a new formula, old-Coke drinkers will then have to make a choice between Pepsi and the new Coke. Pepsi may then win many of these former Coke drinkers. But if you keep your Coke drinkers happy with their original product, the people most likely to try new Coke will be Pepsi drinkers. You should be able to win many of those customers to your new cola and, as a result, increase your total sales.

Option 4 Change the Coca-Cola recipe without telling anyone.

Option 3 will cause more problems than it will solve. The most serious is that the strategy will confuse customers. You already sell Coca-Cola, Diet Coke, and Caffeine-Free Coke. If you put yet another cola on the market, consumers are going to have trouble keeping them straight, and people may tire of trying to sort out the alternatives. "Forget the hassle," they'll say. "I'll just go with Pepsi. At least I know what that is."

In addition, two products that are so similar run the risk of competing for the same customers. As a result, you could end up shelling out a lot of money to introduce a new product that does nothing but steal sales from your original soft drink. Would grocers set aside more shelf space for the new product, or would they simply assign the same shelf space to two products instead of one?

A second cola product would also create an advertising headache. The best way to keep your company visible in a highly competitive world is to have a "flagship" product—one major product with which most people identify your company. For nearly a century, that has been Coca-Cola. With two colas, which do you promote as your image, and how do you do this without slighting your other cola product?

Finally, more products create more difficulties for your bottlers. A bottler could easily set up an operation to bottle Coca-Cola. But if bottlers must produce Coke, Diet Coke, Caffeine-Free Coke, and now new Coke, the process will be far more complicated and expensive.

Therefore, the only way to retain the Coke heritage while moving to improve its taste is to switch to a new recipe secretly. In fact, despite all of the hoopla about "the Real Thing," Coca-Cola's original formula has been slightly altered over the years. Consumers never complained because they did not know about the change.

Other companies commonly make changes in their well-known products without making these alterations public. Heinz, for example, altered its famous ketchup recipe by replacing sugar with less costly high-fructose corn syrup. Heinz never announced the change, and the public never noticed it because people have difficulty detecting such subtle flavor differences.

Tests have shown that image is what influences consumer preferences. For example, people who prefer one brand when they are given labeled samples often choose the opposite when the samples are not labeled. So if you gradually alter the taste of Coke, few people will notice the difference, and you will end up with a more popular taste without sacrificing the Coke image.

YOU ARE THE EXECUTIVE.
WHAT IS YOUR DECISION?

Option 1 Replace the old Coca-Cola product
with a heavily advertised new and
improved Coca-Cola.

Option 2 Keep the old Coca-Cola as your only
regular cola product.

Option 3 Keep the old Coke and bring out the
new formula under a new name.

Option 4 Change the Coca-Cola recipe without
telling anyone.

Coca-Cola chose Option 1.

When he took over the company in the early 1980s, Chief Executive Officer Roberto Goizueta pledged that there would be "no sacred cow in the way we manage our business." Goizueta ignored tradition by borrowing money in order to broaden Coke's business ventures. His aggressive marketing ideas led him to insist that if the research showed that a new formula improved the taste of Coca-Cola, then Coke would change. According to Goizueta, "the brand had a declining share in a shrinking market." He could not sit by and let this continue to happen.

Goizueta dismissed the option of introducing the new formula as a second cola product because he thought that such a strategy would create too much confusion. Instead, he wanted the company's famous name on the company's best cola, which tests had shown to be the new Coke. Goizueta considered the decision "one of the easiest we have ever made."

On April 23, 1985, the company invited the press to gather for what it called "the most important marketing announcement in the company's 100 years." Goizueta introduced the new formula for Coca-Cola, which he said had a "rounder, yet bolder taste." Coke packaged the new product in cans that were marked by a silver stripe. "Thousands of consumers across the width and breadth of this country have told us this is the taste they prefer," said Goizueta of the cola. A huge advertising campaign kicked off the sale of this new product that would entirely replace the old Coca-Cola by the end of the summer.

Coca-Cola chairman Roberto Goizueta (left) and president Donald Keough make a toast with cans of new Coke at the April 23, 1985, press conference where they announced the formula change.

RESULT

The early results supported Goizueta's decision. Within 24 hours of the announcement, more than two-thirds of all Americans were aware of what Coke had done. It was not long before 150 million people tried new Coke, which was an incredibly successful launching. Most reacted favorably, and the product sold well.

But their daring decision soon blew up in the faces of Coca-Cola executives. Loyal Coke drinkers fumed over the loss of their favorite drink and ridiculed the new Coke formula. Within two months, these angry consumers flooded the Coca-Cola Company with nearly half a million letters and telephone calls, demanding the return of the old formula.

Pepsi gleefully declared victory in the cola wars and boasted that "after 87 years of going at it eyeball to eyeball, the other guy just blinked." Comedians such as Johnny Carson and David Letterman poked fun at Coke's decision. The glut of negative publicity soon soured consumers on the new Coke.

In the first week after the product's introduction, a majority of those surveyed thought highly of new Coke. But by July, fewer than one-third approved of the product. This negative response stunned Coca-Cola executives.

After suffering through a three-month nightmare of bad publicity, on July 10, 1985, Coca-Cola brought back the original Coke. Still believing the new Coke was the soft drink of the future, the company referred to the new formula as "Coke" and the original recipe as "Coca-Cola Classic."

The public, however, continued to frustrate the Coca-Cola Company's plan. One survey showed that people preferred Coca-Cola Classic to the new Coke by a two-to-one margin. Although company executives admitted that Coca-Cola Classic was outselling its new product, they insisted those sales would turn around once the fuss had died down. But this did not happen. Instead, major accounts, such as Kentucky Fried Chicken, which had started selling the new Coke, switched back to Coca-Cola

Gay Mullins, president of the Old Cola Drinkers of America and one of the most outspoken critics of the new Coke, rejoices at receiving the first case of Coca-Cola Classic on July 25, 1985.

Classic, and Pepsi began outselling both Coke products combined.

Chief Executive Officer Goizueta stubbornly declared that it was more important that Coke's name be on "its best-tasting product than its best-selling product." But, in 1986, Coca-Cola Classic sold 1.3 billion cases, compared to only 185 million cases of new Coke. The company eventually phased out production of new Coke, which had cost them an estimated $80 million to develop and promote and had subjected them to nationwide public ridicule.

ANALYSIS

Time magazine called Coke's blunder the "most spectacular about-face since Ford walked away from its ill-fated Edsel." Industry analysts noted that the Coca-Cola Company had used flawed research in deciding that old Coke had to go. When they sought customer reactions to their new product, they failed to tell them they were planning to get rid of the original Coca-Cola product. The Coca-Cola Company had spent an enormous amount of money, time, and expertise on developing and promoting the new formula but had failed to measure the strength of customers' loyalty to the old brand name.

Coca-Cola president Donald Keough admitted as much when he said, "We did not understand the deep emotions of so many of our customers for Coca-Cola." Robert Antonio, a sociologist from the University of Kansas, observed that when Coke was replaced, "Some people felt that a sacred symbol had been tampered with."

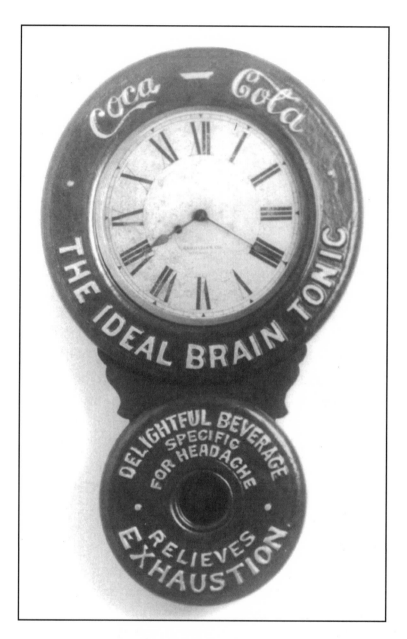

Created originally as a "brain tonic" and a stimulant,
Coca-Cola soon became an American icon and a staple
of the refreshment industry.

Coca-Cola had put itself in an awkward position with its new product. How could it promote a new cola that was more like Pepsi—the very product it had been criticizing in its advertising? Coca-Cola further undermined its efforts by angering fans of old Coke. Instead of getting customers to compare the new Coke with Pepsi, the company's strategy had led them to compare old Coke with new Coke, and the resulting outcry of support for the old Coke came at the expense of the new product.

According to business authors Mark Potts and Peter Behr, "Had its leaders not moved quickly to quell the consumer backlash created by the introduction of new Coke, the company might have been seriously, perhaps irreversibly, damaged." Fortunately, the company recognized and admitted its error. Not only was it able to recover from a major mistake, but it turned the disaster into a success. The widespread, passionate endorsements of Classic Coca-Cola were far more persuasive than any advertising campaign, and Coke got them free of charge. According to one analyst, the blunder "reawakened" loyalty to Coca-Cola.

By the end of the year, Coca-Cola products were increasing in sales at twice the average industry rate. Within two years, Coke products had regained their lead over Pepsi products in grocery stores, and, by the end of the 1980s, Coca-Cola had actually increased its overall market share. Coca-Cola benefited so much from the uproar that some skeptics even wondered whether Coke had planned the whole thing. Although they had not, one marketing executive noted, "Few errors pay off so handsomely."

SOURCE NOTES

Quoted passages are noted by page and order of citation:

pp. 10, 144 (2nd): Robert Heller, *The Decision Makers: The Men and the Million-Dollar Moves behind Today's Great Corporate Success Stories* (New York: Talley, 1989).

pp. 12, 18: Parker Pens promotional materials.

pp. 14, 23 (1st): David Powers Cleary, *Great American Brands: The Success Formulas that Make Them Famous* (New York: Fairchild, 1981).

pp. 23 (2nd), 24: "Parker Jumps," *Business Week*, January 9, 1954.

p. 27: "Writing in Red," *Newsweek*, May 24, 1948.

p. 42 (both): "Research: If the Shoe Fits, Another Winner for Industry," *Newsweek*, April 6, 1964.

pp. 43, 44: "The $100-Million Object Lesson," *Fortune*, January 1971.

pp. 49, 57, 59, 62 (3rd): "Why Boeing Is Missing the Bus," *Fortune*, June 1, 1968.

pp. 58, 61: "Boeing's Future Changes to Cloudy," *Business Week*, March 28, 1970.

p. 62 (1st): Roy Rowan, "Business Triumphs of the '70s," *Fortune*, December 31, 1979.

p. 62 (2nd): Jeremy Main, "Betting on the 21st-Century Jet," *Fortune*, April 20, 1992.

p. 62 (4th): "How to Win by Losing." *Forbes*, June 15, 1971.

p. 75: Andrea Dunham, et al., *Unique Value: The Secret of All Great Business Strategies* (New York: Macmillan, 1993).

p. 79 (both): P. Ranganath Nayak and John M. Ketteringham, *Breakthroughs!* (New York: Rawson Associates, 1986).

pp. 93, 95, 97: Steven Fink, *Crisis Management: Planning for the Inevitable* (New York: AMACOM, 1986).

pp. 101, 103-104, 110: "From Brags to Riches," *Business Week*,
February 22, 1982.

pp. 102, 114 (both): Robert F. Hartley, *Marketing Mistakes* (New York:
Wiley, 1989).

p. 104 (2nd): "Crash of a Computer Pioneer," *Macleans*,
September 26, 1983.

pp. 119, 121, 128 (both), 132 (both): Peter C. Reid, *Well-Made in
America: Lessons from Harley-Davidson on Being the Best* (New York:
McGraw-Hill, 1990).

pp. 144 (1st and 5th), 146: "Coke Tampers with Success," *Newsweek*,
May 6, 1985.

pp. 144 (3rd), 150 (1st): Mark Potts and Peter Behr, *The Leading
Edge: CEOs Who Turned Their Companies Around and How They
Did It* (New York: McGraw-Hill, 1987).

p. 144 (4th): Roger Enrico and Jesse Kornbluth, *The Other Guy Blinked*
(Garden City, N.Y.: Doubleday, 1986).

pp. 148 (1st), 150 (2nd): Thomas Moore, "He Put the Kick Back into
Coke," *Fortune*, October 26, 1987.

p. 148 (2nd, 3rd, and 4th): "Coca-Cola's Big Fizzle," *Time*, July 22,
1985.

BIBLIOGRAPHY

"Boeing's Future Changes to Cloudy." *Business Week*, March 28, 1970.

Cleary, David Powers. *Great American Brands: The Success Formulas that Make Them Famous*. New York: Fairchild, 1981.

"Coca-Cola's Big Fizzle." *Time*, July 22, 1985.

"Coke Tampers with Success." *Newsweek*, May 6, 1985.

"Coke's Man on the Spot." *Business Week*, July 29, 1985.

Colander, Pat. *Hugh Hefner's First Funeral and Other True Tales of Love and Death in Chicago*. Chicago: Contemporary Books, 1985.

"Crash of a Computer Pioneer." *Macleans*, September 26, 1983.

Dunham, Andrea, et al. *Unique Value: The Secret of All Great Business Strategies*. New York: Macmillan, 1993.

Enrico, Roger, and Jesse Kornbluth. *The Other Guy Blinked*. Garden City, N.Y.: Doubleday, 1986.

Fink, Steven. *Crisis Management: Planning for the Inevitable*. New York: AMACOM, 1986.

"From Brags to Riches." *Business Week*, February 22, 1982.

Fucini, Joseph, and Suzy Fucini. *Entrepreneurs: The Men and Women behind Famous Brand Names and How They Made It*. Thorndike, Maine: G. K. Hall, 1985.

Guzzardi, Walter. "Big Can Still Be Better." *Fortune*, April 25, 1988.

Hartley, Robert F. *Marketing Mistakes*. New York: Wiley, 1989.

Heller, Robert. *The Decision Makers: The Men and the Million-Dollar Moves behind Today's Great Corporate Success Stories*. New York: Talley, 1989.

Hendon, Donald W. *Classic Failures in Product Marketing: Marketing Principles Violations and How to Avoid Them*. New York: Quorum, 1989.

"The House Falls In on the SST." *Newsweek*, March 29, 1971.

"How to Win by Losing." *Forbes*, June 15, 1971.

Kehrer, Daniel M. *Doing Business Boldly: The Art of Taking Intelligent Risks*. New York: Times Books, 1988.

Main, Jeremy. "Betting on the 21st-Century Jet." *Fortune*, April 20, 1992.

Mayer, Martin. *Making News*. Garden City, N.Y.: Doubleday, 1987.

"The Mighty Pen." *Time*, September 26, 1955.

Moore, Thomas. "He Put the Kick Back into Coke." *Fortune*, October 26, 1987.

Nayak, P. Ranganath, and John M. Ketteringham. *Breakthroughs!* New York: Rawson Associates, 1986.

"The $100-Million Object Lesson." *Fortune*, January 1971.

"Parker Jumps." *Business Week*, January 9, 1954.

Potts, Mark, and Peter Behr. *The Leading Edge: CEOs Who Turned Their Companies Around and How They Did It*. New York: McGraw-Hill, 1987.

Reid, Peter C. *Well-Made in America: Lessons from Harley-Davidson on Being the Best*. New York: McGraw-Hill, 1990.

"Requiem for a Polymer." *Time*, March 29, 1971.

"Research: If the Shoe Fits, Another Winner for Industry." *Newsweek*, April 6, 1964.

Rowan, Roy. "Business Triumphs of the '70s." *Fortune*, December 31, 1979.

Serling, Robert. *Legend and Legacy: The Story of Boeing and Its People*. New York: St. Martin's Press, 1992.

"Synthetic Rival for Leather." *Business Week*, October 5, 1963.

Taylor, Graham, and Patricia Sudnik. *DuPont and the International Chemical Industry*. Boston: Twayne Publishers, 1984.

Tedlow, Richard S. *New and Improved: The Story of Mass Marketing in America*. New York: Basic Books, 1990.

"Why Boeing Is Missing the Bus." *Fortune*, June 1, 1968.

"Writing in Red." *Newsweek*, May 24, 1948.

INDEX

111, 112, 114;
development of, 100-101;
market for, 101, 102, 103,
104, 105; price of, 101,
103, 106, 114
computer, portable. *See*
computer, personal
Computerland, 101
Concorde, 50
Congress, U.S., 58, 61, 126
consumer research. *See*
market research
Control Data, 100
Corfam: compared to
leather, 33, 34, 35, 39, 40,
43; development of, 29,
33; failure of, 42-44;
manufacturing of, 29, 33,
34, 36, 37, 40, 41, 42;
test marketing of, 36, 40
corporate executive,
responsibilities of, 7, 9, 10
Crisis Management, 95
cyanide, 84, 88, 90, 94, 96
CYBER computer, 100

Davidson, Arthur, 116
Davidson, Walter, 116
Davidson, William, 116
Decision Makers, The, 10
Deming, W. Edwards, 123-
125
disk drive, 101
Duofold fountain pen, 18,
26
DuPont: decision of, on
production of Corfam, 33,
34-44; and development
of synthetic leather, 29,
32, 33; history of, 30-31;
losses of, with Corfam,

42-44; and nylon, 30-32,
33, 37

Edsel, 7, 8, 148
Eisenhower, Dwight D., 15
electronics companies, 65,
71, 76. *See also* Sony; JVC
Eversharp, 24, 28
Executive 1, 110, 111, 112,
114
Executive 2, 110, 112

FBI, 84, 85
Fink, Steven, 94, 95
Food and Drug
Administration, 85
Forbes, 62
Ford, Gerald, 57
Ford Motor Company, 7,
148
format, VCR, 65, 67-68, 69,
71-73; Betamax, 75, 76,
77, 78, 80; VHS, 76-78,
79
Fortune, 57, 59
Foster, Larry, 97
fountain pen, 11, 13, 14, 17,
18, 19, 20, 24, 27, 28;
market for, 14, 19

Gee, Edwin, 44
General Electric, 76
Goizueta, Roberto, 137,
144, 145, 146, 148
gunpowder, 30

Harley, William, 116
Harley-Davidson Motor
Company: changes in
management of, 128, 129,
130, 132; history of, 116-

117; image of, 117, 119-
120, 121, 131, 140;
Japanese competitors of,
115, 117-119, 120, 123,
125-126, 128, 130, 132;
product quality of, 115,
116, 117, 119, 120, 122,
128
Hayes, Arthur, 85
Heinz, 142
Heller, Robert, 10
Honda motorcycles, 117,
118, 119, 120, 123, 125-
126, 128, 130
Hubbard, Eddie, 47
Hutchinson, Ron, 128

IBM, 103, 104, 105, 106,
107, 110, 111, 112, 113,
114
Ibuka, Masuru, 64, 74, 75

Japanese: computers, 106,
110; electronics
companies, 65. *See also*
Sony, JVC; management
techniques, 123-125;
motorcycles, 115, 117,
118, 120, 122, 125, 128,
130. *See also* Honda
Johnson, Edward, 82
Johnson, James, 82
Johnson, Robert, 82
Johnson, Robert Wood, 86,
87, 89
Johnson & Johnson: history
of, 82, 83; recall of
Tylenol by, 86-89, 93-94,
97-98; relationship of,
with McNeil Consumer
Products, 82, 84, 88-89,

94, 98; reputation of, for
integrity, 82, 86, 90, 95,
97; and Tylenol
poisoning, 81, 83-84, 85-
94, 96
Jotter ballpoint pen, 25
jumbo jet, 53, 54, 57, 59, 60.
See also 747
JVC, 65, 70, 71-73, 76-78,
79

Kawasaki, 118
Kennedy, John F., 51
Kentucky Fried Chicken,
147
Keough, Donald, 145, 148
ketchup, 142
keyboard, computer, 101

Lawson, William, 41, 43
leather: natural, 32, 33, 34,
35, 36, 37, 39, 42, 44;
synthetic, 29, 32-33, 34,
36, 37, 39, 42
leather-tanning industry, 37,
38, 39, 42, 44
Letterman, David, 146
Lewis, James, 96
Lockheed, 54
Lucky Curve fountain pen,
13
Lynch, Charles, 38

McDonald's, 135
McNeil Consumer
Products, 82, 84, 88-89,
94, 98
Magnavox, 76
Main, Jeremy, 62
management techniques,
123-125

market research, 53; on cola
beverages, 135, 136, 138,
142, 144, 148; on Corfam,
34, 36, 40, 43; on VCRs,
69, 70, 73, 76, 79. *See also*
test marketing
Matsushita, 65, 71
monitor, computer, 101
Montgomery Ward, 8
Morita, Aiko, 64, 74
motorcycles: Harley-
Davidson, 115-117, 118-
122, 126, 128, 130-131,
132; Honda, 117, 118,
119, 120, 123, 125-126,
128, 130; Japanese, 115,
117, 118, 120, 122, 125,
128, 130
Mullins, Gay, 147

Newsweek, 27
Nikolitch, John, 38
Nixon, Richard, 57
nylon, 30-32, 33, 37

Old Cola Drinkers of
America, 147
Old Hickory plant, 40, 41
Osborne, Adam, 100-101,
102, 103-104, 109, 110,
111, 112, 113
Osborne Computer
Corporation: competitors
of, 99, 103, 104-105, 108,
110-111, 112, 114; history
of, 99-101; losses of, 110-
111, 112, 114; pricing
policy of, 101, 103-104,
105, 114; role of, in
development of personal
computer, 101-102, 103,

109
Osborne 1, 101, 102, 105,
107, 110, 112, 113, 114

Panasonic, 65
Paper-Mate, 25
Parker, George, 12-14, 22,
23
Parker, Kenneth, 22, 23, 27
Parker 51, 14, 15, 20
Parker Pen Company: and
ballpoint pen, 16-23, 25,
27, 28; and fountain pen,
11, 13, 15, 18, 19, 20, 26,
27, 28; history of, 12-14,
15; reputation of, for
quality, 14, 17, 19, 20, 21,
23, 25, 27, 28
"Pepsi Challenge," 135
Pepsi-Cola: competition of,
with Coca-Cola, 133,
134-135, 136, 137, 138,
140, 141, 146, 148, 150;
market of, 135, 136, 140
picture tubes, television, 64
plastic, 31
Potts, Mark, 150

quality control, 122-123,
125, 129
Quasar, 65

Radio Shack, 103
RCA, 10, 76
"Real Thing, the," 134, 138,
140, 142
Red Barn, 46
research and development,
30, 33, 34, 37, 43
Rockwell, Norman, 139

Sears, 8
SelectaVision, 10
Senate, U.S., 59, 62
Serling, Robert, 51
747, Boeing, 56, 57, 58-60,
61, 62
707, Boeing, 47-49, 57
shoes, 29, 39; Corfam, 33,
34, 35, 36, 37, 40, 42, 43;
leather, 33, 34, 35, 36, 37,
40, 42, 43; vinyl, 33, 34,
37, 40, 42, 43
software, computer, 101-102
Sony: and Betamax VCR,
75, 76, 77, 78, 79, 80;
history of, 64, 68, 74;
relationship of, with JVC,
65, 71-73; role of, in
development of VCR, 63,
65, 67-73, 75-76
Sprite, 140
SST (supersonic transport),
50-53, 55, 57, 59, 60, 62.
See also supersonic aircraft
stockings, nylon, 31, 32, 33
Sturgis, South Dakota, 121,
131
supersonic aircraft, 49, 50-
53, 55, 57, 58, 59, 60, 62.
See also SST

Takano, Shizuo, 79
Teerlink, Rich, 132
television, 64, 65
test marketing, 36, 40, 136
Time, 148
Tokyo Telecommunications
Engineering Company,
64. *See also* Sony
transistor radios, 64
Tylenol: manufacturing of,

82-83, 84, 88; poisoning
of, 81, 83-84, 86-91, 94;
recall of, 86-89, 93-94,
97-98; tamper-resistant
packaging of, 85, 86, 89,
91, 94, 95

videocassette recorder
(VCR), 63; Betamax, 75,
76, 77, 78, 80;
development of, 65-67,
69, 75; formats of, 65, 67-
68, 69, 70, 71-73, 76;
VHS, 76-78, 79
Video Home System (VHS),
76-78, 79
video systems, home, 10, 63.
See also videocassette
recorder
videotape machine, 65, 66,
70
vinyl, 33, 34, 37, 42, 43
Vixen, 110, 112

Webster, William, 85
Westervelt, G. C., 46
Wilson, Thornton, 56, 62
World War I, 8
World War II, 8, 15, 16, 47,
124

Yamaha, 118

ABOUT THE AUTHOR

NATHAN AASENG is an award-winning author of over 100 fiction and nonfiction books for young readers. He writes on subjects ranging from science to business, government to sports. Aaseng's books for The Oliver Press include *Great Justices of the Supreme Court*, *America's Third-Party Presidential Candidates*, *Genetics: Unlocking the Secrets of Life*, *You Are the Supreme Court Justice*, *You Are the President*, *You Are the President II*, *You Are the General*, *You Are the General II*, *You Are the Senator*, and the upcoming titles, *You Are a Member of the Jury* and *Treacherous Traitors*. He lives in Eau Claire, Wisconsin, with his wife and children.

Photo Credits